OPTIMIZING
WORK PERFORMANCE

Recent Titles from Quorum Books

OPTIMIZING WORK PERFORMANCE

A Look Beyond the Bottom Line

MARTIN MORF

Quorum Books

New York • Westport, Connecticut • London

Library of Congress Cataloging-in-Publication Data

Morf, Martin.
  Optimizing work performance.

  Bibliography: p.
  Includes index.
  1. Personnel management.   2. Employee motivation.
3. Work environment.   4. Ability.   I. Title.
II. Title: Work performance.
HF5549.M62   1986   658.3'1   85-23232
ISBN 0-89930-143-6 (lib. bdg. : alk. paper)

Library of Congress Catalog Card Number: 85-23232
ISBN: 0-89930-143-6

First published in 1986 by Quorum Books

Greenwood Press, Inc.
88 Post Road West, Westport, Connecticut 06881

Printed in the United States of America

The paper used in this book complies with the
Permanent Paper Standard issued by the National
Information Standards Organization (Z39.48-1984).

10 9 8 7 6 5 4 3 2 1

To my parents

Contents

PART IV. QUALITY

Exhibits

Preface

In a nutshell: this book is about basics. It is in tune with the "back to basics" movement most familiar to the public in the discussion of American education, yet equally important in the debate about the strengths and weaknesses of American management in the face of overseas competition. The "reinvented corporation" of John Naisbitt and Patricia Aburdene, the "vanguard corporation" of James O'Toole, and the just-plain-excellent companies of Thomas Peters and his associates are all described as paying meticulous attention to the basics.

But while there is a consensus that managers must once again focus on "the basics," there is less-than-complete agreement on what the basics are. A relatively traditional school of thought says they are "to produce excellent products and provide high-quality services." A more emotive group of management consultants focuses on the *how* rather than the *what* and embraces with tears of joy both workers and customers, who apparently played no role of consequence in the number-oriented past two decades. Still others argue that managers need a broader education, including some exposure to the liberal arts, to make higher quality decisions that take into account not only their organizations but also the society on whose welfare that of their own organization depends.

The basics this book looks at are of a fourth type: They consist of certain facts, relationships, principles, guidelines, and sometimes even theories that provide some understanding of what determines how people do their work and of what the consequences of their efforts are. These generally applicable fundamentals can allow us to develop useful strategies and solutions for the specific situations that face us and to critically evaluate strategies and solutions offered by others. This book is meant to be more like a fishing rod than a fish.

My intent is to introduce in a step-by-step fashion the broad concepts that underlie the decision making going on every day in every work organization, and to do this so gradually that the reader reaches the top without really noticing the steps. Whether that intent has been realized remains to be seen; what is certain is that the steps on the ladder to "enlightenment" are motivation → ability → competence → working conditions → performance → consequences of performance.

To the end of keeping things simple, patterns that might introduce some order are exploited fully. The reader will thus repeatedly encounter a number of dichotomies: person versus environment, macro level versus micro level of analysis, analytical versus holistic, and behaviorist versus cognitive approaches. I don't apologize for the somewhat compulsive reliance on what patterns I could detect. Cleanliness may be next to godliness, but orderliness cannot be too far behind.

A caveat may be in order here. My formal training focused on the psychology of personality. I am not a specialist in industrial and organizational psychology, management, education, economics or other disciplines touched on in this book. The net I cast is a wide one, and this raises the problem of accuracy. The original sources were not always available and the reader may find that the occasional error managed to elude me.

This book assumed a definite form during a sabbatical granted by the University of Windsor and spent in part at the Swiss Federal Institute of Technology in Zürich. My colleagues there, in particular Eberhard Ulich and Felix Frei, effectively challenged my most fundamental assumptions. My former graduate students Catherine Miller and Rick Hackett faithfully offered helpful feedback over the years. University of Windsor colleagues Henry Minton of the Department of Psychology and Megeed Ragab of the Faculty of Business have offered advice and constructive criticism on several chapters. The many and detailed comments of the students in my Psychology of Work course inspired considerable rewriting. This does not exhaust the list of people who contributed in some way to this effort and whose help is also acknowledged. The actual writing, editing and proof-reading would not yet be completed without my assistant, Kay—a real pro.

OPTIMIZING
WORK PERFORMANCE

1.

Understanding Work Behavior

The pace of business is usually hectic. Managers, entrepreneurs, human resource professionals, industrial and organizational psychologists, and the average employee don't typically have time for academic discussions, for pursuing issues in depth, or for looking beyond the immediate trouble spot. They have to keep other people happy: The boss is pounding the table; the shareholders are muttering. Their attitude is pragmatic. They rely on techniques that have worked before. Often they opt for the quick fix, the miracle technique advertised in the current bestsellers and on the management seminar circuit.

All this frantic activity, this hectic pace, this pragmatic striving for what appears to matter most—productivity—leaves little time for finding out what is really going on. The human need to understand and to see the big picture gets short shrift. Few stop to reflect on what it is they are doing or on the meaning of their work and that of their subordinates. Many of us may be frantic workers, but few of us pursue the subject of work in depth or on a broad front.

TOWARD A DEEPER AND BROADER UNDERSTANDING OF WORK PERFORMANCE

This book addresses two main points concerning the neglected big picture. The first point is that optimizing work performance must be a central concern because of its implications for the quality of life. This implies that work performance does not only matter because of short-term productivity considerations. Sometimes optimal work performance involves sacrificing productivity gains to attain other objectives: higher quality, increased goodwill on the part of clients, more careful maintenance of human resources and machinery. The second point is that steps taken to optimize work performance must be based on an understanding of fundamental concepts and processes pertaining to human resources in the form of motivation and ability and to the work environment in the form of the job itself and the physical and social conditions in which it is embedded.

Depth

Depth of understanding implies a focus on general principles, that is, on fundamental concepts and important relationships among them. These general principles have what psychologist Paul Meehl (1972) called "second-order relevance." Their usefulness, often overlooked by people in a hurry, is that they allow one to derive solutions for a wide range of problems, not just the one that currently looms ahead and absorbs all attention. Relying on broad concepts of second-order relevance, it may be possible to formulate solutions, effective interventions, or techniques that have first-order relevance. The capacity to develop such first-order solutions is more useful than actual procedures and techniques that have worked somewhere and somehow for reasons no one understands.

An approach characterized by depth is almost by definition philosophical in nature. It is the philosopher who penetrates beneath the surface and identifies the basic issues to which our concerns are related. The philosophers who seem to have addressed people's concerns about work more enthusiastically and vigorously than anyone else are Karl Marx and Friedrich Engels.

The thinking of Marx and Engels is not viewed with heartfelt approval in the American business world. It certainly requires one to distinguish between Marxist ideology on one hand and Marxist philosophy and psychology on the other. That may not always be easy, but the former usually leads to vague and often absurd assertions about true democracy reigning to the east of the Iron Curtain and loud rhetoric about the "peace-loving countries" of the Warsaw Pact. Marxist ideology is of no interest here.

What is of interest is Marxist psychology because, more than any other body of thought, it addresses itself to the central issue of work. While we define psychology as the study of behavior, the Russians define it as the study of work behavior.

Engels asserted bluntly that "labour created man himself" (1976, 170), and Soviet psychologist Aleksei Leont'ev dutifully elaborates that thought: "The cause underlying the humanising of man's animal-like ancestors is the emergence of labour and the formation of human society on its basis" (1981, 204).

According to Leont'ev, there are three kinds of activity: play, learning, and work. The first two prepare the developing child for the third and most important one. Work activity is the typical activity of adult life and it has important effects on the worker: New motives or intentions are formed; new competencies are acquired. Work and learning thus go hand in hand.

Leont'ev argues that activity, in effect work activity, consists of actions which in turn consist of operations. Corresponding to these three levels of activity are motives, goals, and concrete working conditions. The motive may be to contribute to the socialist state or to the enterprise or to become rich, the goal might be to attach 100 locks to 100 chassis before the end of the shift, and the concrete working condition that is most salient may be a conveyor belt that moves one chassis per minute past the worker.

According to Leont'ev, a characteristically human trait is the ability to pursue specific goals that appear to conflict with one's broader motives. As early as the hunter-gatherer stage, it may have been the role of some to chase game away by making noise. Such action did not immediately contribute to the work activity of obtaining food. The goal seems to contradict the motive. But these beaters knew that their "comrades" were on the other side of the clearing ready to do their part in a larger, cooperative effort. Action and hence work activity are conscious and social.[1]

Work activity is also the construct which receives the undivided attention of Winfried Hacker (1978), an East German psychologist following in the tradition of his Russian and senior colleagues. Hacker concentrates on basics not only in the sense that he focuses his text on work activity, but also in that he seeks to link the myriad forms of work activity to a few basic psychological processes—pertaining to the energizing and execution of activity—that regulate it. While one may not agree with his offhand dismissal of Western psychology, one is likely to admire his efforts to push work activity into the center of psychology as the chief means of personality development as well as of a society's productivity, and to link the findings of the psychology of work to the broader philosophical and psychological concepts of Leont'ev and his Soviet colleague Sergei Rubinstein (1977).

Scope

Scope implies inclusiveness or breadth of interest, concern, and knowledge. For example, it implies an interest not only in determinants of behavior which can be manipulated to increase productivity, but also in effects of work behavior on the worker's personality and on the quality of life offered by society-at-large. It also implies an interest not only in environmental determinants of behavior which to the pragmatic mind seem the most manipulable and hence useful in optimizing productivity, but also in the person, that is, in biological and personal (i.e., conscious, internal) determinants of behavior. A broad scope or broad awareness is a precondition for developing balanced outlooks on important issues such as determinants versus consequences of work behavior and the role of person and environment in determining work behavior.

Determinants and Consequences

Scope or breadth implies awareness of a large range of determinants and effects of work behavior, scientific and professional interest in the values of not only business, but also labor, and interest not only in the sphere of work, but also in the sphere of personal life. The basic dichotomy here is that of determinants and effects: In general, business and the work sphere are associated with determinants, while effects are of greater concern to labor and to people in their personal life roles as consumers and citizens.

An awareness of effects is particularly important. As Ronald Burke (1982) points out, industrial and organizational psychologists have been far less interested in the effects, other than on productivity levels, of work behavior than in its determinants. That is what one would expect if indeed the business of America is business. Pragmatic businesspersons want what will work in their quest for higher productivity. Hence the focus is on the determinants of performance and productivity. The consequences of performance are generally of interest only from the point of view of productivity. Direct and intrinsic effects on the worker or more subtle effects on the quality of life offered by a community or society are not in the forefront of concerns.

Person and Environment

Our attitudes toward the roles of the person and the environment in accounting for work behavior are somewhat contradictory. Privately, we tend to blame people when things go wrong. The official emphasis is, however, on the role of the environment. As far as the social scientists are concerned, the environment is a far more important determinant of human behavior than the person.

Both the private and official positions are extremes; behavior is obviously a function of interactions between person and environment. But the extremeness of the official position is the more serious of the two since it constitutes the conventional wisdom transmitted to those being trained for careers in business, administration, and the professions. At least officially, the graduates of America's business schools and graduate psychology programs are likely to believe that behavior is almost entirely a function of the environment, that people can invariably be "helped" and that organizational functioning can invariably be improved by identifying things that will work as rewards, and by making these rewards contingent on desired behavior.

A certain amount of pragmatic simplification characterizes both the conservative and everyday view that people are to blame when things go wrong, and the liberal and scientific view that work performance is basically a result of a properly designed environment. Instead of adopting a complex interactionist perspective that considers both the environment and the person, we officially adopt the bolder and simpler position of environmentalistic behaviorism. This choice simplifies matters by avoiding the complex "person" construct and allows one to go ahead and start manipulating behavior without further ado. Like the one-sided endorsement of business values and, more generally, the emphasis on determinants, the tendency to attach overwhelming importance to the environment at the expense of the person indicates a lack of scope.

There is a great deal of confusion concerning person and environment in psychology generally. The comments on depth suggest that the roots of basic concepts must be pursued and that in the process these concepts could be linked to general psychological principles, ideally perhaps to basic perceptual and learning processes established in the psychological laboratory. The confusion on person and environment suggests the same principle on a broader scale: There is a need for a broader, more general perspective. The philosophers may have to help us analyze person and environment and the relationships between them.

The main source of confusion is the tendency of psychologists to perceive one issue, that of person versus situation, when there are really three. In the context of these three issues it becomes possible to diagnose the liberally educated and fashionable manager's and the modal industrial or organizational psychologist's pragmatic simplification more precisely as *immediate-environment monism.*

This condition is marked by a tendency to reject the person construct in every way in which it can manifest itself: as a set of personal determinants emanating from within the person's consciousness, as a set of biological or genetic determinants, and as a set of traits or broad personality characteristics. As the immediate-environment monists see it, the only thing that seems to determine behavior is the immediate environment. Even the idea that the past environments of childhood, adolescence, and early adulthood might have helped to shape basic personality characteristics is viewed with suspicion.

Rejection of personal determinants. The first issue pits the idea of "choice" against the idea that personality and behavior are mechanistically determined in all respects and at all times. This is the famous debate between French existentialist Jean-Paul Sartre and American psychologist B. F. Skinner (Skinner, 1971). It should be noted that the idea of choice can assume different forms (e.g., the strong form of personal freedom and indeterminism, and the more circumspect form of "personal determinants," that is, internal determinants that cannot be completely reduced to biological or at least fairly stable dispostions) (Hospers, 1967).

Skinner argues that everything we do, including our most "creative" and "heroic" acts, is strictly the result of an environment that reinforced some behavior patterns and failed to reinforce others. So you wrote a beautiful and even widely read poem? So you courageously expressed an unpopular view or pointed to powerful politicians with their fingers in the till? You can cease patting yourself on the back because you simply emitted behaviors that your environment reinforced in the past. As Skinner sees it, choice is in no way involved in the behavior of which you are so proud and for which you are prepared to take the credit. There are no such things as freedom, dignity, courage, or virtue.

Sartre, viewing the world through the fears and anxieties of specific individuals such as his character Roquentin in the novel *Nausea* (1949), that is, relying on subjective rather than objective evidence, constructs a universe of cowards ("salauds") who do not make courageous choices and heroes who do. Skinner and Sartre talk about two different worlds, the worlds revealed by objective and subjective evidence.

Rejection of biological determinants. Even if personal determinants are rejected, controversy continues. There now arises the second issue: that of biological versus environmental determinants. This is the old nature versus nurture debate. The person appears here as nature, and it has taken a beating. Skinner (1957) here too is one of the chief spokesmen for the environment. Noam Chomsky (1957, 1972), postulating innate dispositions to use language in certain ways, is his adversary on this issue. Unlike the first issue, this one deals with something in the past rather than current behavior, with the question of how personality develops.

The rejection of biological determinants has had important implications in the context of ability. Among psychologists, reaction has been sharp and hostile to colleagues maintaining that different people have different talents or, more contentiously, that different people have different IQs in large part because of different genotypes. The anger and vituperation that greeted the work of Hans Eysenck (1971), Richard Herrnstein (1973), and especially Arthur Jensen (1969) are a reflection of the dogma that the environment is *the* shaper of personality and behavior.

Rejection of traits. The rejection of the person construct even includes past interaction between biological and environmental determinants resulting in relatively stable dispositions called traits. Here we have the traits-versus-environment issue addressed by Walter Mischel (1968, 1984). Like the choice-versus-mechanism issue it deals with present behavior, but like the nature-versus-nurture issue it has implications for what happened, or rather did not happen, in the past.

The term *interactionist position* emerged from the trait-versus-environment debate and described the belief that neither traits nor environment accounts for much variance in behavior. According to the interactionist view, behavior is almost invariably a function of specific dispositions elicited by specific environments. In statistical terms, if persons and environments are the factors of a 2×2 design, the main effects mean squares reflecting the role of either person or environment are minimal and the interaction mean square reflecting the importance of the role of person and environment as an interacting system is substantial.

The currently predominant view in social science is certainly interactionist. However, the interaction often is perceived to be that between an unimportant person and a very important environment. In short, we still need to wrestle with the question of balance between environmental and person factors in our account of work behavior.

The dialectical position of Marx and Engels is relevant here. Marx saw class conflict—the contradiction between the interests of the bourgeoisie and those of the proletariat—as the motor of historical development. This basic postulate lies at the root of Soviet psychology largely for reasons of dogma, but the dialectical paradigm and the emphasis on contradictions and change manifest themselves in many other ways.

What is of interest here is the dialectical relationship between the person and the environment summed up in Marx's assertion that "labour is a process in which both man and nature participate. . . . [A]cting on the external world and changing it, . . . [man] at the same time changes his own nature."[2]

This dialectical fusion of person and environment in work activity assumes concrete form in the efforts to redesign jobs or, to use the European term, to humanize work. One example of such efforts is the work of Felix Frei, Werner Duell, and Christof Baitsch (1984) which grew out of the Marxist tradition as well as Western efforts to raise the quality of working life (Emery and Thorsrud, 1976; Davis and Trist, 1974). The practical consequences of their work include interventions to change working conditions in a way that allows them to foster competence and personality growth.

In the United States, similar work is going on. It differs from what the Europeans are doing in two important ways, however. Its theoretical basis is far less ideologically tinged. Instead of Marxist philosophy, the Americans rely on in-depth analyses of a more objective nature. In many ways the conclusions reached by such American psychologists as Albert Bandura and Mischel converge with those of Hacker and Leont'ev. Mischel (1973, 1984) argues that the relationship between the person and the environment is not a one-way relationship in which the environment shapes the person, but a reciprocal relationship in which the person also affects the environment not only in the obvious sense of having a physical impact on it, but also by filtering it, interpreting it, forming expectations about it, and so forth. Bandura (1978) seems to go a step further and to consider behavior as not only a consequence, but also as a determinant, of both person and environment. He thus allows for the usually neglected possibility that work is important as a personality-developing activity.

The second way in which American approaches to redesigning or designing work differ from the European ones is in their pragmatism. Probably the best-known work in the area is that of Richard Hackman and Greg Oldham (1980). It is based on a model that is simple and useful, but these authors saw no compelling need to relate it to a broader, theoretical framework such as that provided by the social learning theories of Bandura and Mischel.

These two characteristics of American work in the area are clearly related. The Europeans pay the price of subjectivity and gain the benefit of a certain commitment that makes them look at the problem of designing work within a broad theoretical framework. The question of the meaning of work for the worker is on their minds. American psychologists, on the other hand, are not distracted by ideological niceties. They generate sound scientific analyses which, however, are not usually carried over into the arena of applications with noteworthy passion.

TWO SYSTEMS APPROACHES TO WORK

Work is a set of activities. Depending on the point of view, it is a set of activities engaged in by one person, by a group of workers, by the personnel of an entire work organization, or by the national workforce.

The activity constituting work can be regarded as throughput of a system. The system can be anything from John Doe's shoveling coal to the national economy. Whatever the system of interest, its input variables (i.e., the determinants of work) are likely to include abilities, skills, motivation levels, available technology, and managerial styles. The output variables or effects of work include the goods produced and the services provided, the pollution generated and the depletion of resources caused.

The systems approach can be rather vague and general. There are very few things that are not "systems" in some sense of the term. The advantages of the systems approach, however, include its flexibility and its ability to take into account simultaneously many and complex relationships. One way in which the flexibility manifests itself is in the idea that there is always a hierarchy of systems. As noted above, we can approach work in terms of a hierarchy of systems ranging from very small subsystems, like the individual worker, to large suprasystems, like the national economy.

Focus on the Work Organization

As the term *industrial and organizational psychology* indicates, the system central to the analysis of work is typically thought to be the work organization. This is because it forms a distinguishable unit of elements that must complement each other. For example, the best workers cannot produce in a work organization that is unable to organize its projects and provide the tools and the environment required to do the work.

The work organization consists of subsystems. One way to look at it is to focus on its divisions or departments: Marketing, finance, and production then become subsystems of interest. Another way is to focus on its employees, ranging from the chief executive officer to the employees on the front line behind the counter in the bank, on the assembly line in the plant, or in the aisles of the department store. In short, the work organization works, and so do its departments and individual employees.

The work organization is part of a suprasystem: of an industry, of the business sector or techno-economic structure, and ultimately of society. The ultimate suprasystem of interest is the world as a whole, consisting of the world's population in its gobal environment, but the suprasystem of most direct concern in an analysis of work is likely to be the national society, in this case the society of the United States. While the boundaries between national societies are becoming more permeable in the age of telecommunications and computerized databanks, the national society remains a distinct entity characterized by its own laws reflecting its own background and values. We are thus likely to judge the effects of workers, defined here as all those who work, by the changes they produce in the quality of life offered by American society.

Focus on the Work Situation

A second approach, the one generally taken here, focuses on the work situation rather than the work organization as the system of primary interest. One can look at the work situation in two quite different ways. What might be called the unstructured work situation consists of one or more workers in a particular work environment. An example of such an unstructured work situation might be a group of five postal clerks in a small post office, supervised by a postmaster, manning two wickets and sorting mail that arrives from and is sent to a central post office facility twice a day.

But we can also look at the work situation with a particular framework in mind. One very useful and basic framework is the dichotomy of person and environment we encountered in the preceding discussion of scope as an aspect of understanding work behavior. If we structure the work situation somewhat by dividing it into the worker and the work environment, we have what will be called here the structured work situation.

In this structured work situation, the work environment is seen from the "typical" worker's point of view and includes his or her co-workers. The typical worker who appears in this way of looking at the work situation is not to be confused with a particular worker. Whatever statements we make about the effects of the typical worker on the environment, or about the effects of the work environment on the typical worker, would in general apply to all of the five workers forming part of the unstructured work situation in the small post office.

OVERVIEW OF THE STRUCTURED WORK SITUATION AND ITS CONTEXT

There are thus at least two reasonable approaches to the study of work. One can focus on the system constituted by the work organization or on the system consisting of the typical worker and his or her work environment. Although these two approaches are complementary, this book adopts the second one as its basic approach.

This choice of approach is based on two assumptions. The first is that the analysis of the typical individual worker can tell us much about the nature of work that we have tended to overlook in recent decades because of our tendency toward "immediate-environment monism." We have seen that among social scientists, though not necessarily in other sectors of the American population, the individual has not been of great interest. The emphasis has been on the environment or at least on the system of which individuals are parts, on aggregates or groups of people like management teams and unions. In the debate between Skinner and Sartre, Skinner and the environment have emerged triumphant while Sartre and the individual person making choices have been relegated to the drawer labeled "quaint notions." Like most imbalances, this one is probably not healthy.

The second assumption underlying the focus on the structured work situation and the individual worker is that it is generally wise to proceed from smaller systems to larger ones, that is, from the bottom to the top of the hierarchy of subsystems, systems, and suprasystems rather than vice versa. A detailed understanding of specific effects of individual workers on themselves, their work environment, and their general environment, and of the effects of their environments on the workers, is likely to be helpful in obtaining a better understanding of the larger system—the work organization—of which these workers are parts. Of course, it is often the case that a larger system is quite well understood while some of its constituents remain utter mysteries. The cell was adequately described in textbooks before anyone knew the structure of the DNA molecule. But unless special circumstances indicate otherwise, the strategy of proceeding from smaller systems to larger ones appears to have merit.

These two assumptions lead to the basic framework for approaching work which is depicted in Exhibit 1-1. In the overview of the work process depicted in this exhibit, the worker looms large and so do the effects of work behavior on the environment. The diagram reflects the important, albeit obvious, fact that work behavior is the result of the interaction between personal or organismic (left-hand side of diagram) and environmental (right-hand side) factors. This interaction is a theme that provides an important organizing principle of the discussion of almost all major topics in this book. Especially in the contexts of motivation and ability, the focus will first be on the person, then on the environment, and finally on the complex interaction between the two.

Exhibit 1-1
The Worker, the Work Environment, and the General Environment

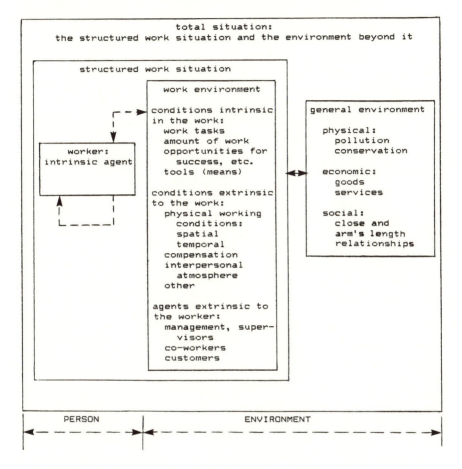

```
                        total situation:
        the structured work situation and the environment beyond it

        structured work situation

                        work environment

            ┌ ─ ─►  conditions intrinsic      general environment
            ╎       in the work:
            ╎         work tasks                 physical:
            ▼         amount of work               pollution
    worker:           opportunities for            conservation
    intrinsic agent     success, etc.
                        tools (means)             economic:
                                                    goods
            ▲       conditions extrinsic          services
            ╎       to the work:
            ╎         physical working           social:
    L ─ ─ ─ ┘           conditions:                close and
                        spatial                    arm's length
                        temporal                   relationships
                      compensation
                      interpersonal
                        atmosphere
                      other

                    agents extrinsic to
                    the worker:
                      management, super-
                        visors
                      co-workers
                      customers

    ┆    PERSON       ┆              ENVIRONMENT
◄── ─ ─ ─ ─ ─ ─ ─ ─►┆◄─ ─ ─ ─ ─ ─ ─ ─ ─ ─ ─ ─ ─ ─ ─ ─ ─ ─ ─►
```

Some Relationships Between Worker, Work Environment, and General Environment

The various aspects of the work environment can be classified in different ways (e.g., Hacker, 1978; Herzberg, Mausner, and Snyderman, 1959; and Schneider and Locke, 1971). Perusal of earlier classification systems suggests the three main categories indicated in Exhibit 1-1: conditions intrinsic in the work, like the tasks constituting the job; conditions extrinsic to the work, such as physical working conditions; and agents extrinsic to the worker, like managers and supervisors.

These main categories are essentially those of Joseph Schneider and Edwin Locke. But Schneider and Locke are concerned with the work situation rather than merely the work environment. The work situation, as defined here, includes the work environment as well as the worker. To accommodate the latter, Schneider and Locke have a fourth main category consisting of a single job dimension: an agent intrinsic in the worker—the worker him- or herself. She could be a factory worker, an office worker, a manager, or even an entrepreneur. She contributes to the work situation primarily two things of interest: motivational dispositions and abilities.

The worker's needs determine which of the potential rewards offered by the work environment are actually perceived to be rewards. These perceived rewards are goals, and the combinations of needs and goals, which like the goals themselves are formed through learning, are motives. These motives form the foundation of work behavior. Without them there is little behavior of consequence, and that includes little acquisition of ability.

Ability is the second necessary condition of performance supplied by the worker. The term is used here broadly to refer to what a person can do and it includes aptitudes (what a person is capable of learning), skills (specific abilities, usually involving the perceptual-motor system), and knowledge (the cognitive basis of making choices, information).

The worker and the work environment, constituting the structured work situation, are part of a larger entity, the total situation which also includes the broader environment beyond the work situation. This broader environment contains a multitude of elements. One way to introduce some order among them is to distinguish between the broader environment's physical, economic, and social aspects. We will see that important effects of work, effects that go beyond the traditional bottom line, pertain to this broader environment.

This brings us to the effects that the worker, the work environment, and the general environment have on each other. The worker engages in work behavior that affects both the work situation and the general environment. This work behavior may fall into the category of performance or it may be work behavior other than performance.

If the outcomes offered by the work environment are contingent on performance, then performance actually produces these outcomes, be they money, indicators of success including promotions, or verbal recognition. Performance may thus cause the work environment to provide greater and more numerous rewards or it may actually change the particular worker's work environment if the rewards consist of greater responsibilities or promotion to a corner office.

The second major class of effects of performance is those that influence the general environment beyond the immediate work situation. These primarily affect the satisfactions of the beneficiaries rather than the performers of work. The high performer may generate less pollution or may conserve resources, that is, may affect the physical environment. As the philosopher Alfred North Whitehead wrote: "The administrator with a sense for style hates waste; the engineer with a sense for style economises his material'' (1929, 23). Performance is also likely to raise the quality of the economic environment by resulting in more goods of higher quality and in services that serve their purpose. The civil servant whose performance is high will do more than pass the buck and grunt unintelligibly. High performance may also improve our social environment. The competent therapist can improve close relationships with other family members; the competent social worker may organize government housing tenants to mount effective campaigns to bring their problems to the attention of their landlord.

Work behavior other than performance—managers, industrial and organizational psychologists, and human resource professionals think here mainly in terms of negatives like absenteeism, job turnover, lack of punctuality, accident-producing behavior, and sabotage—is distinct from but related to performance. It is distinct from performance in a very obvious way when rewards are not contingent on performance. The worker may like going to work because the job offers social contacts and an escape from an unsatisfactory home life precisely because it does not call for high performance and allows ample time for long coffee and lunch breaks. Work behavior other than performance is related to performance in that the worker who is not on the job, otherwise engaged when on the job, or even determined to reduce productivity is not able to perform or is performing poorly.

So much for some of the effects of the worker on the work environment and the general environment. How is the worker in turn affected by these environments? The work environment affects the worker by providing rewards that reduce needs (produce satisfaction). In fact, the common element of performance and other work behavior is that they are both engaged in to obtain rewards of some kind.

The effects of the general environment on the worker are much more complex. It is not pleasant to work in a polluted industrial area that puts out more smoke and gaseous emission than useful goods. The economic environment, the techno-economic structure in which we work, may be conservative or liberal; it may treat the worker as a human being or as part of the machinery. It is likely to espouse old-fashioned industrial values like hard work and reliability, but it may insist on them flexibly or rigidly. Finally, there is the social environment, essentially what sociologist Daniel Bell (1976) calls the "culture." This culture is the realm of liberty in which we live, the world of TV entertainment, Saturday afternoon baseball, rock music, and the plethora of popular magazines and tabloids. But it is also the world of education, ranging from acquisition of basic social skills to appreciation of Plato and Hegel. It is likely to instill self-oriented values that conflict with those of the techno-economic structure, but it may do so to a greater or a lesser extent.

The general environment also affects the work environment. For example, a work organization that ignores the values propagated by the general environment is likely to offer fewer rewards to the worker than one that takes these values into account and institutes job design efforts that seek to accommodate them where possible. While the workplace is changing, it has been democratized less slowly than the general environment—in particular, less slowly than the social environment beyond the structured work situation. There are reasons for this. For example, production may require quick decisions. But the social environment has been producing expectations and demands on the part of workers that can be met by introducing alternate work forms such as autonomous work groups and participative decision making.

Feedback Effects of Work on the Worker

One important process taking place in the work situation that is often overlooked is that work behavior affects the worker herself. Exhibit 1-1 allows for such feedback effects. The aspect of the worker most frequently influenced by performance is ability levels. New skills are developed and new knowledge is acquired in the very process of doing a job, particularly when it is well designed and well done.

Performance may also affect personality in general. These broader effects seem of greater interest in cultures other than that of the United States. Hacker's (1978) authoriative analysis of work, widely read on both sides of the Iron Curtain, contains a chapter on the effects of work on personality. Hacker emphasises that he is writing about work under "socialist conditions of production," but Christof Baitsch and Felix Frei (1980), building on Hacker, have reported detailed procedures for designing jobs that allow workers to develop skills and abilities as an integral part of the work process in a free-enterprise context.

On the other side of the globe, in Japan, there are psychologists who believe that even monotonous work can have benefical effects on the performer. Jyuji Misumi (1982), for example, suggests that Japanese workers often regard even routine work as a learning experience. They do so, according to Misumi, in the Buddhist tradition which prescribes many hours and days of floor sweeping and rice boiling as a means to self-enlightenment. In a similar vein, according to Frank Gibney (1982), Shichihei Yamamoto writes: "Zen and the 'economic animal' concept come from the same source. . . . By Zen standards [work] amounts to something like religious training. . . . Thus when a manufacturer makes good products he is showing one face of the Buddha . . . to bring profit to the world. When a salesman makes his rounds, he is on pilgrimage" (pp. 21-22).

UNDERSTANDING PERFORMANCE IN TERMS OF MOTIVATION, ABILITY, AND THE WORK ENVIRONMENT

Exhibit 1-1 depicts the "total situation" with which this book is concerned. A certain structure is imposed on the elements of the work process depicted in this general schema by the basic postulate:

$$Performance = Worker \times Work\ Environment$$

In other words, performance requires both a person and an environment, and they must interact in some way. Since it is primarily the worker's motivational dispositions and abilities that are relevant in the context of work, we can write:

$$Performance = (Motivation \times Ability) \times Work\ Environment$$

Since the product of motivation and ability is what is usually called competence, this is equivalent to writing:

$$Performance = Competence \times Work\ Environment$$

All that these statements tell us is that performance involves three things—motivation, ability, and suitable working conditions—and that if any one of these three things is absent (i.e., if its value is zero), work performance will also be zero. In practice, things are somewhat more complicated; for example, work performance is usually considered to be "a function of" rather than "equal to" the product of the various terms in the equations above.

The postulate *Performance = Competence × Work Environment* has appeared in the literature in many forms and in a way sums up the body of knowledge offered by industrial and organizational psychology (Campbell and Pritchard, 1976; Vroom, 1964). It is a postulate about performance, the topic of the discipline and of this book and the thing many employees and most managers seek to optimize. As shown in Exhibit 1-2, the structure of the entire book is based on it.

Part 1 deals with motivation, the engine without which not much of interest pertaining to work performance happens. Next, the abilities of workers are introduced; they combine with motivation to yield competence, the subject of Part 2. Competence, however, can only manifest itself in the right work environment, that is, under the right working conditions. Just as ability is the new element that leads from motivation to competence, so the work environment is the new element that leads from competence to performance. The latter, although the subject of the book as a whole, is specifically focused on in Part 3. It is also the immediate bottom line of interest to managers and usually to workers. Part 4 looks at some of the effects of performance on the performing worker, on the work environment, and, above all, on the broader environment and society-at-large. All of these effects have implications for the ultimate bottom line: the quality of life of both workers and the beneficiaries of their work.

Exhibit 1-2
Relationships Between Main Concepts of the Book

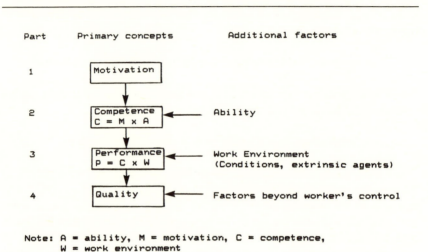

Note: A = ability, M = motivation, C = competence,
      W = work environment

NOTES

1. This interpretation of Leont'ev (1981) is influenced by a number of additional sources. Translation and verification posed some problems, and my account is subject to further clarification.

2. Cited from McLennan (1975, 38). The point is clear, in spite of the fact that "nature" first refers to the environment and then to the person.

PART I.

MOTIVATION

2.

The Motivated Person and the Motivating Environment

In one of his short stories, the Swiss writer Friedrich Dürrenmatt (1952) humorously points to the obsessive work habits of his countrymen. A train has entered a tunnel. The tunnel turns out to be endless and it gradually curves toward the center of the earth. Passengers and crew have to hang on for dear life as the train hurtles downward at ever-increasing speed, but the train conductor dutifully continues to fill out his numerous schedules.

Alexander Solzhenitsyn (1963), in his novel *A Day in the Life of Ivan Denisovich*, describes how a work gang of brutalized, cold, and hungry concentration camp inmates suddenly experiences a surge of energy and of pride that makes it build the tallest and straightest wall on the work site.

Both Dürrenmatt's train conductor and Solzhenitsyn's prisoners exhibit unusual degrees of motivation to do a job right regardless of the consequences. They may be fanatics or fools, but in a way we admire them for exhibiting a high level of work motivation.

Such motivation exists not only in literature. Before the advent of the railroad, John Thompson crossed the forbidding Sierra Nevada dozens of times on his skis to deliver the mail from the East to isolated California. Ten or twenty years ago, high in the Swiss Alps, the lucky climber may have come across a hut kept by a woman who insisted on serving coffee as if she were hosting a bridge club meeting in a suburb of Zürich. Although the water had to be carried a distance of several steep miles, and in spite of the fact that she had no refrigerator, she served coffee with cream and in porcelain cups. In Nagoya, Japan, there is at least one innkeeper who drops everything to take his foreign guest personally through a near-typhoon to a restaurant which will serve the dishes the guest wishes to taste, and who will spend a sleepless night if the guest does not come back smiling.

The nineteenth-century postman, the woman of the mountains, and the Nagoya innkeeper are all heroes in the battle to raise the quality of life. In the spirit of Marshall Pétain, who said, "They shall not pass" in the face of the Germans attacking Verdun in World War I, they say, "Service shall not decline."

These examples suggest that the critical aspect of work performance and work quality is motivation. That piece of insight is not immediately useful, however, because motivation is clearly a fuzzy concept. It can denote the area of psychology studying motives; it can also refer to a cluster of motives. Thus we speak of the psychology of motivation and the motivation of individuals to work, to develop, to win, to become rich.

What is important for our purposes is what different meanings of the term *motivation* have in common. Both of the above uses of the term share a concern with the question of what makes people expend energy in particular directions, and both, more generally, deal with the changing aspects of personality, with what is called *personality dynamics*. The word *motivation* is derived from the latin *movere* (to move), and the term *dynamics* comes from the Greek word *dynamos*, familiar from such derivatives as *dynamo, dyne* (the physicist's unit of work), and *dynamite*.

Motivation is clearly related to ability. Not only is motivation required to acquire abilities, but abilities may also be determinants of motivation. For example, the sense that one is growing and becoming more capable can be a powerful motivating force. This close relationship means that it is useful to look at the two together in establishing the larger picture, the context of motivation. That context, as shown in Exhibit 1-1, is the relationship between the person, as a worker who brings motivation and ability to the job, and the environment which provides stimuli and conditions eliciting motivation and ability.

Exhibit 2-1 provides an overview of the interaction between the worker and the environment over time. Both motivation and ability are characteristics of the worker which are in large part the result of past or current environments. The past environment of early childhood inculcates needs to do one's duty, to satisfy customers, to create things that will last and that will be beautiful. The present environment, as we have seen, may or may not elicit these needs and may or may not provide the means to do a good job. Exhibit 2-1 thus shows the developing individual and the environments that affect the developmental process whose end product is the adult worker facing specific tasks in the current environment.

The interaction between person and environment is complex. The strategy used here is to deal first with the person and then with the environment. Both motivation, in Chapters 2 to 4, and ability, in Chapters 5 and 6, will be approached with a useful fiction in mind: the fiction that the roles of the person and of the environment can be separated. Only after the roles of the person and the environment have been examined separately will the more complex interplay between the two become the subject of interest.

Exhibit 2-1
Person-Environment Interaction over Time

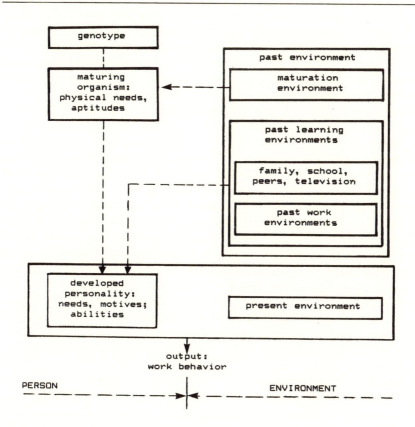

PERSON AND ENVIRONMENT IN THE CONTEXT
OF MOTIVATION

A Philosophical Perspective: Rousseau Versus Hobbes

A fundamental assumption underlying this first chapter on motivation is that the profusion of theories of motivation relating dispositions of the person to the rewards offered by the workplace boils down to two basic classes shown in Exhibit 2-2: theories based on Jean Jacques Rousseau's optimistic conception of man's proclivities to do the right thing in a natural environment, and his pessimistic condemnation of the "civilized" environment; and those based on Thomas Hobbes' pessimistic assessment of human nature and his reliance on civilization to prevent presumably brutish individuals from doing the wrong things. This dichotomy is developed in some detail by Curt Tausky (1978).

According to Rousseau, "Nothing is more gentle than man in his primitive state, as he is placed by nature at an equal distance from the stupidity of brutes, and the fatal ingenuity of civilized man" (1961, 198). Hobbes (no date) could not disagree more. Among his best-known utterances are "every man is enemy to every man" (p. 81) and "the life of man [is] solitary, poor, nasty, brutish and short" (p. 81). Even when these assertions are not taken out of context, when they are read with Hobbes' qualifiers, they do reflect a pessimistic view of human nature.

As Tausky points out, the followers of Rousseau think of the average member of the workforce in terms of Douglas McGregor's (1957) Theory Y, as "social man" or as "self-actualizing man," happily executing work because it satisfies higher level social needs: the needs to develop, learn, and "grow." "Treat workers as mature adults," they say. "Do not interfere in their activities on the job, let them set their own pace, make their own decisions." The Hobbesians—and most employers are Hobbesians at heart—see the worker more in terms of McGregor's Theory X, as "economic man" or "instrumental man," ready to work for concrete rewards like money, status, and power. In the Hobbesian view, people will not expend energy and make an effort unless the environment induces them to do so by either dangling carrots in front of their faces or swishing a stick in the general vicinity of their backsides.

Exhibit 2-2
Two Basic Models of Man

Source:	Hobbes "The natural state of men, before they entered into society, was a mere war...a war of all men against all men."	Rousseau "...nothing is more gentle than man in his primitive state..."
Emphasis:	On the "civilizing", i.e., restraining, environment	On personal growth and development
McGregor:	Theory X	Theory Y
Specific variants (and organizational theories):	Economic man (scientific management) Instrumental man (contingency theory)	Social man (human relations) Self-actualizing man (human resources)

A Psychological Perspective: Cognitive Versus Behaviorist Positions

Cognition refers to perceptual and thought processes, and these processes give rise to a person's goals, expectations, perceptions, intentions, and purposes. The cognitive psychologists tend to pay considerable attention to these products of cognition. In other words, cognitive psychologists are relatively person-oriented. They take off the lid and look into the mind, exhibiting a keen interest in its processes, in the throughput of the system called "person" or "mind." Goals and related constructs are seen as determinants of behavior, as explanatory constructs. Two of the major figures in the cognitive camp are Kurt Lewin and Mischel. It is important to note that neither of them sees behavior as a function of the person. Both see it as a function of the person *and* the environment. It is only in comparison with behaviorism that cognitive psychology can be considered relatively person-oriented.

The cognitive school stresses perceptions of positively or negatively evaluated aspects of the environment. For example, in the area of work motivation it is not the objective job characteristics, the objective features of the wider work context, or the objective outcome of work performance that matters. What matters are the perceived characteristics and outcomes, the perceived rewards. An employee may be working contentedly to earn a salary of $18,000 until it is discovered that the co-worker at the next desk earns $18,500.

What people subjectively perceive as desirable or undesirable depends on their needs. Needs are satisfied by objects, events, and conditions. To Lewin, the salient characteristic of these aspects of the environment is their valence, the value assigned to them by the motivated person. The valence of an object or event can be positive or negative; if it is negative we want to avoid it. A low performance appraisal from the supervisor would fall into this category, and so would a dismissal notice. Since needs are normally cyclical, the valence of objects and events can increase and decrease. A steak is likely to have a positive valence to the person who has not eaten all day, but it may be nauseating after an eight-course meal.

Because they attach significance to such distinctly human attributes as complex cognitive processes and goals, purposes, and so forth, cognitive psychologists tend to study humans rather than the rats and pigeons traditionally preferred by the behaviorists. In general, their psychology is more complex than that of the behaviorists. They argue that in human beings consciousness is a determinant of behavior and that this means that human subjects must be studied and that constructs beyond those of the behaviorists are required to formulate adequate and useful explanations of human behavior.

We have encountered the behaviorists in the discussion of environmental determinants of behavior and personality in Chapter 1. They are inclined to have little use for the notion of personality in the traditional sense of a large and identifiable entity. Instead, they attribute behavior to stimuli that elicit it and to reinforcers that strengthen it. They acknowledge a contribution of the organism as the processor of input (sensations) and generator of output (responses), but they treat it as a machine that contributes physical imbalances and neural circuits to the total process generating observable behavior. The organism is seen as a black box transforming inputs into outputs in accordance with simple laws that can be established by empirical observation. The mind is not seen as something that has to be opened, examined, and understood. It is a Pandora's box, best left unopened.

That people report having goals, and that they themselves experience the influence of their own goals, cannot be denied by the behaviorists. But they treat goals and related entities as epiphenomena, as notions that are of little importance. They see them as covert behaviors that may be worth explaining, not as entities that are needed to explain behavior.

The behaviorists thus avoid words and concepts referring to mental processes and they regard as meaningless assertions like "drivers stop for red lights because they expect a ticket and demerit points if they don't." "Expectation" is a cognitive concept which the behaviorists believe is somewhat mysteriously invoked to explain behavior in spite of the fact that more parsimonious and complete explanations in terms of drive, reinforcement, and incentives are available. Furthermore, to an orthodox and rigorous scientist like the average behaviorist, there is something uncanny about goals because they are teleological rather than causal concepts and seem to suggest that behavior is somehow determined by the future rather than by the past.

Those who think in terms of goals and purposes do not share this interpretation. To them what lies in the future is the attainment of the goal. But while this attainment lies in the future, the goal itself is a factor that has its roots in the past and its effects in the present. But the fact remains that it is much easier to fit concepts like stimulus, response, reinforcement, and drive into a scientific and mechanistic schema of the world.

The behaviorists also feel uneasy with concepts like goals and expectations because these concepts are not scientific in the sense that the data from which they are inferred are ultimately not replicable and verifiable. They can only be approached by means of subjective reports. Behaviorism is associated with a hard-nosed scientific attitude, and exponents of it like John Watson and B. F. Skinner chafe at the idea of evidence that cannot be replicated.

The behaviorists are thus not interested in subjectively perceived rewards. They are interested in the actual and objective rewards, such as a food pellet, and their incentive values, such as the incentive value of a food pellet for a hungry rat. Rewards are generally defined as stimuli that can reduce needs, that is, can produce drive reduction. Needs are said to affect the incentive value of potential rewards. How they do that can be studied objectively in the laboratory. For example, if the rat works hard to attain a food pellet, the incentive value of the pellet is obviously high. The question then becomes, What objective conditions can raise or lower it? The behaviorists thus see no need to resort to the notion of subjectively assigned or experienced valences.

Behaviorism originated and developed largely in the animal laboratory. It is a tenacious school of thought that clings mightily to the belief that a scientific explanation of behavior must above all be as simple as possible, must make as few assumptions as possible. Its strength is, in other words, its parsimony.

The features of these opposing schools of thought are listed in Exhibit 2-3. It is difficult to choose between them. As long as the behaviorist explanation of events in a particular domain is satisfactory, its simplicity usually makes it the preferable one. However, it does not seem able to explain work behavior adequately, at least not without becoming labored and as complex as cognitive theory. Usually our approach to behavior in general and work behavior in particular is cognitive. The main use of behaviorism is in its challenge to justify every assumption involving the contents of the human mind, and to refrain from lazily attributing behavior to them when that is not necessary.

Exhibit 2-3
Cognitive and Behaviorist Perspectives

Cognitive perspective	Behaviorist perspective
Focus on the person and the person's consciousness	Environment as determinant of behavior and personality
Focus on organism's throughput	Organism as black box transforming inputs into outputs
Goals, perceptions, expectations as explanatory constructs	Goals, etc., viewed as covert behaviors to be explained
Proponents: Lewin, Mischel	Proponents: Watson, Skinner
Focus on subjectively perceived rewards and incentives	Focus on objectively existing rewards and incentives
Needs as determinants of perceived rewards and incentives	Needs as tensions reduced by rewards and incentives
Origins in human psychology	Origins in animal psychology
Defended as useful, realistic, and true	Defended as parsimonious

The reader may wish to speculate on the similarities between the Rousseau versus Hobbes dichotomy and the cognitive versus behaviorist dichotomy. Do Rousseau and the cognitive psychologists share a certain liberal attitude toward assumptions about human nature and human information processing? Do they share an open mind toward the possibility that the individual, the person, the worker plays an important role in determining behavior? Is Hobbes similar to the behaviorists in his tough-minded emphasis on the environment?

THE MOTIVATED PERSON

A focus on the person implies a focus on the biological and personal determinants introduced in Chapter 1, on the Rousseauian emphasis on basically good human nature, and on a cognitive approach that considers the goals and expectations of people to be important determinants of their behavior. We will first look more closely at the biological and then at the cognitive aspects of the person.

Needs

What we would ultimately like to have is a theory of motivation that explains why people do things. But that is a very ambitious goal, and it is a good idea to start with something more basic than full-fledged theories. Scientists start out with observations, but soon these observations lead them to formulate concepts and constructs, for example, abstractions like the concept *horse* which refers to what real horses have in common. To explain motivation, psychologists have formulated a variety of constructs. Among these the most fundamental is the construct *need* at which we must take a closer look.

The Biological Basis of Motivation

The most basic motivational constructs are obviously biological in nature. Furthermore, the most important among these biological constructs is the notion of *physical need*. Motivation is always rooted in needs, and at least the obviously biological needs are fairly concrete and clearly identifiable imbalances of the body. The body needs above all oxygen, water, and food. The need for oxygen is unusual because it does not by itself generate clear-cut signals that something is lacking. Somehow, nature saw fit not to encourage the development of a warning system. The reason may be that a lack of oxygen is almost always accompanied by an excess of carbon dioxide which builds up in the lungs unless we breathe, and this excess produces strong reflexes that in turn cause us to gasp for air. In the case of other physiological needs, the body signals the imbalances directly.

For example, when food is not forthcoming, the acid content of the stomach increases and produces hunger pangs.

Thus needs are imbalances or tensions which are signaled, either directly or indirectly, to our consciousness. The unpleasantness associated with them is what makes us move. But while biological or physical needs account for discontent, restlessness, and generally aimless activity, they do not explain specific behavior patterns. Why does the hungry traveler feel pushed toward the part of the strange town where he is most likely to find a restaurant? Why does the thirsty TV watcher head for the refrigerator and open a beer?

For a long time, instincts were invoked to explain why people and animals act the way they do. But the method of explaining some pattern of behavior by attributing it to an instinct was circular and not parsimonious. It was circular because it simply removed the need to explain from the behavior to the instinct. For example, sex differences in attitudes to children were attributed to the strength of maternal and paternal instincts, but no one was sure how these instincts functioned and developed.

The instinct explanation was not parsimonious because the complexity of human behavior required a vast array of instincts. As many as 6,000 were proposed at one point (see Bernard, 1924). This confusing multitude of suggested instincts led to a reaction and to the introduction of the concept *drive*. Instead of 6,000 explanatory constructs there was now only one.

According to Clark Hull (1943), for example, drive is a single state that may result from many different imbalances. In Hull's view, the lack of water, of food, of sexual gratification all produce the same internal drive state that makes the organism restless, diffusely discontented, and ready to undertake steps to remedy the imbalance. The hungry rat will run around more vigorously in the activity wheel—a device measuring activity level—than a smugly satiated one. On the level of human social behavior, downright frenzy may result when the needs of a large segment of society are not met. The French were hungry in 1789. The Russians were both hungry and tired of serving as cannon fodder at the front in 1917. Needs and the activity they generate are what the word *drive* refers to. Those in the grip of drive are driven or pushed by an unpleasant internal state.

Psychological Needs

Although physical needs are the root of motivation, we rarely think of hunger or thirst as our reasons for doing something. There is still plenty of food and water in North America, and most physical needs are taken care of before they become powerful motivating forces. What we usually cite as the cause of our actions are psychological needs.

One must distinguish clearly between two types of theories about psychological needs: those theories that assume that need reduction or drive reduction can completely account for motivation and those that assume that some motivation has nothing to do with drive reduction. The two types of theories differ in that the first postulates only deficit needs (needs resulting from some tissue deficit such as lack of water) while the second type of theory postulates both the usual deficit and some particularly human growth or neurogenic needs.

Psychological deficit needs. The traditional deficit theories have the advantage of being parsimonious. In other words, they explain motivation with few assumptions. Psychological needs are assumed to be elaborations of physical needs and they are assumed to have developed through learning.

The first step in explaining typical behavior is to formulate the psychological needs most likely to underlie it. This will lead to a list of psychological needs that constitute a rudimentary motivation theory. Campbell and Pritchard (1976) have distinguished between *content theories* of motivation which postulate a set of particular needs or environmental factors that appear useful in explaining human activity, and *process theories* which explain how the person's needs and the environment's salient features interact to produce motivated behavior. In this section dealing with the motivated person, and not yet with the interaction between person and the motivating environment, it is content theories listing a set of needs that are of particular relevance.

One of the oldest and most influential among these need theories is that of Henry Murray, a personality theorist who intensively studied a group of about 50 normally adjusted subjects by means of interviews, projective psychological tests, and other methods. Murray (1938) reported the work he and his colleagues had done at the Harvard Psychological Clinic in a book titled *Explorations in Personality*. This classic of the personality literature discusses a host of psychological needs. Among these are well-known ones like the needs to affiliate with others, to be taken care of, to take care of others, to dominate, to be aggressive, and, best-known of all, the need to achieve.

Murray's needs illustrate the fact that psychological needs are not as different from physical ones as one might think. It is only because we do not know enough to show concretely what physical mechanisms underlie them and how they have evolved from physical needs that we treat them as if they were not really physical. The word *psychological* in this context is thus a tacit admission of ignorance.

It is reasonable to surmise that everything about living organisms is ultimately material, or physical. That would include the subjectively perceived personal determinants and the sense of freedom and responsibility reported by many people. Murray's need to achieve, for example, could be rooted in a lack of parental solicitude in infancy that raised the threatening possibility that food and water might not be forthcoming at the appointed times. Perhaps parental solicitude increased whenever the infant performed a new feat, such as gurgling two recognizable syllables in a row, and perhaps this solicitude acted as a reinforcer to strengthen achievement-oriented behavior because it was tied to the satisfaction of physical needs.

But there are behaviors, particularly human behaviors, that do not lead to drive reduction in an obvious way. These behaviors include activity for its own sake, such as repeated manipulation of aspects of the environment that do not lead to the reduction of a clearly identifiable physiological drive or psychological deficit. They have to do with curiosity, exploratory behavior, aesthetic preference for complex rather than simple stimulus patterns, and *epistemic* ("knowledge-producing") behavior.

Scientists like parsimony and tend to cling to drive reduction theories because an explanation of motivation in terms of one basic principle is simpler than one that involves other principles as well. For this reason, Daniel Berlyne (1960) tried to explain curiosity, exploratory behavior, and other behaviors of similar nature by means of a modified drive reduction theory.

Berlyne's modification hinges on his distinction between arousal potential and arousal of the reticular activation system of the brain. A monotonous situation, according to Berlyne, is low in arousal potential but the boredom it produces is itself a drive, a high arousal state of the reticular activation system no different from that produced by a challenging or exciting situation. The level of arousal of the bored worker on the auto assembly line may not be different from that of the hunter aiming at an angry grizzly.

The relationship between reticular arousal and the arousal potential of a situation can thus be represented by an inverted U-curve. Situations that have low or high arousal potential elicit a high level of reticular arousal, while situations that are neither boring nor exciting produce a low level. According to Berlyne, behavior that seems designed to increase drive thus in fact reduces the reticular arousal produced by boredom.

Growth needs. But is drive reduction really all there is? For decades, the dominant view shared by behaviorists like Hull and psychoanalysts like Freud has been that drive reduction is indeed all there is. This view has increasingly come under attack. At least two schools of thought have emerged in psychology that challenge the assumption that all motivation is based on drive reduction. Their adherents argue that not all needs are organic, physiological, or viscerogenic. Not all needs are based on some deficit, some tissue imbalance that generates activity to correct the situation. Both of these schools have at least one important root in the thinking of existentialist philosophers who stress the human capacity to make free choices and assume the responsibility for them, and the human need to be true to oneself—in Sartre's word, to be *authentic.*

The first of these schools of thought postulates what Richard Lazarus and Alan Monat (1979) call the "force-for-growth school." Its best-known exponents are probably Alfred Adler, Carl Rogers, and Abraham Maslow—all of whom built their theories of personality around the core concept of self-actualization. In their view, this high-level psychological need is not something to be reduced or associated with an undersirable state of tension. On the contrary, it is something that is satisfying, that energizes the individual and that directly, not through tension reduction, leads to what Maslow called "peak experiences."

Maslow (1954), for example, addresses himself to the possibility that there are two kinds of quite distinct needs: deficit needs and growth needs. There is little argument about the nature of the deficit needs. They are the familiar needs we have discussed so far, the needs that involve either a clearly physical or at least a psychological state of imbalance which the organism is disposed to rectify. Maslow considers the growth needs to be typically human, linked to self-actualization, and as forces that impel the organism to seek stimulation rather than a reduction of stimulation, to seek challenges, learning environments, and opportunities for self-expression and self-development.

Maslow also postulates that needs form a hierarchy ranging from physical needs to needs for safety, love and belonging, and self-esteem, and ultimately to the self-actualization needs. This postulate implies that higher level needs do not manifest themselves until the needs at lower levels are satisfied. Thus it may be that the American craving for "growth experiences," for the many kinds of therapies offered, and for religious experiences are a function of the affluence of the 1960s and 1970s, and that they may weaken in the wake of recession and a lower level of affluence.

This force-for-growth school of thought has something theological about it. If you have faith in "the force" it is a meaningful concept that will affect your behavior. But it is probably very hard to convince those who lack the faith that this force is one to be reckoned with.

The second school of thought that seeks to go beyond drive reduction is less speculative and more specific and analytical. Its proponents in psychology include Robert White and Richard deCharms, and its central concepts are those of effectance and personal causation. This school postulates two kinds of needs: the familiar viscerogenic needs that originate in nonneural tissue deficits, like hunger that leads to easily fathomed behavior, and the neurogenic needs that originate in the nervous system, which do not lead to consummatory acts like eating and which sometimes cause the organism to seek to increase a need rather than to decrease it. These neurogenic needs are closely related to competence and will come up in Chapter 7 in a more detailed discussion of White's concept of competence.

Goals

Motivation theory that relies on the idea of need can go only so far. It can explain energy, tension, dissatisfaction, and restlessness. But a motive is more than energy; it also causes energy to be expended in a certain direction, to attain certain things. We usually call these things "goals" if we are person-oriented cognitive psychologists, "incentives" if we see them as part of the environment. Incentives are best thought of as rewards that have some incentive value that enables them to attract the attention, and cause changes in the behavior, of people.

It has been said that a motive is a need plus a goal. That would imply that it has both a biological component or a psychological component that originated in a biological component, and a cognitive one. The focus of this section is on the latter.

The concept *goal* is a much more controversial notion than that of *need*. Two questions are of particular interest here. First, to what extent is a goal an aspect of the person? Just where do we draw the dividing line between goal and incentive? We speak of "our" goals but claim to strive for things out there in the environment, for example, a salary increase, a bigger office, an office with a rug. Certainly broad goals of achievement, success, and wealth are part of our personality. They are stable and general and linked to other personality elements like the need to achieve.

But we also formulate some of our goals on the spur of the moment as a result of an incentive beckoning in our environment. For example, the ticket to the baseball game may generate the goal to finish work early to get to the game on time and use the ticket. Like specific attitudes and momentary interests, these short-term goals are more a function of the current environment than of the person. In the context of this section, it is the general goals that are more clearly an aspect of the person and are of relevance here.

A second question is whether goals are necessary to explain behavior. We have seen in the preceding discussion of cognitive versus behaviorist views that the answer seems to be "yes." Although the behaviorists offer ingenious arguments and teach us to be cautious about making too many assumptions, cognitive theory relying on concepts like *goal* is very influential in the explanation of work motivation.

THE MOTIVATING ENVIRONMENT

Rewards

The previous section has addressed the problem of why, in the same situation, one worker will enthusiastically expend energy in handling the tasks at hand while another will lurk about on the sidelines watching the clock. In this section we look at the other side of the coin: Why does the same worker hustle like a beaver in some situations and loll about like a recently fed lion in others? We have seen that a focus on the environment may mean emphasis of environmental determinants of personality and behavior—perhaps a Hobbesian emphasis on the "good" environment that will restrain us and civilize us—and that it definitely implies a behaviorist rather than a cognitive approach. It may also mean a focus on the "content" of the environment, a content theory listing environmental features that motivate workers. One of these is that of Herzberg, Mausner, and Snyderman (1959) discussed in Chapter 3.

The woman of the mountains serving decent coffee regardless of profit, the train conductor filling out his forms and schedules regardless of the impending crash, Ivan Denisovich and his crew building the highest and straightest wall regardless of their slave masters' ingratitude—all are individuals whose motivation originates in large part within themselves. When we compare them to the majority who in similar circumstances would throw in the towel, we are struck by the great differences among persons and by the importance of personality.

However, this does not mean that the environment is unimportant. What goals in the person's consciousness are to the cognitive psychologist, rewards or incentives offered by the environment are to the behaviorist. Some behaviorists may go overboard, but there are reasons for stressing the role of the environment. There seems little doubt that most of us do things most of the time because the environment encourages us to do them. That is not the issue. The issue is whether the environment plays the dominant or even exclusive role all of the time, whether it is never a matter of goals and always a matter of rewards.

Roles of the Work Environment and the General Environment

Exhibit 1-1 suggests that it is not only the work environment, but also the more general environment (including the culture), that is important in determining the values and motives the worker will bring to the job. The work environment is described in the exhibit as consisting of three categories of factors: conditions intrinsic in the job, conditions extrinsic to the job, and agents extrinsic to the worker. All of these act on the worker by providing rewards or punishments. High performance on the job is typically associated with a sense of satisfaction. The challenge and responsibility of the job that makes this satisfaction possible is intrinsic in the job itself. Extrinsic conditions, such as a bonus, or extrinsic agents, such as the supervisor who dispenses hearty and public approval, provide other examples of rewards.

Among various factors of the broader environment producing powerful effects on motivation, the culture is probably the most important. For most of the eighteenth and nineteenth centuries in Europe and America, the culture fostered the so-called work ethic, a set of values designed to make people work hard. An entirely different culture produced different values in the 1960s: The "letting go" ethic of the counterculture generated a lofty attitude toward "merely competent" workers who did not understand that life involves growth, experimentation, and above all "doing one's thing." In Japan, many different cultural currents, such as *bushido* and the traditions of the rice culture, generate a workforce dedicated to the success of its employers. In many socialist countries the absence of incentives and official discouragement of acquisitive enterprise generate resignation and sometimes downright stupor instead of high levels of work motivation.

Some work environments and cultures are thus clearly more motivating than others. This is important because it raises the possibility of changing environments to optimize work motivation. The culture is usually beyond the reach of such intervention, but changes can be effected in the work environment. The effects of these changes are always, however, the result of the interaction of worker and work environment. This interaction is the subject of the next chapter.

3.

The Interaction Between Motivated Person and Motivating Environment

In Chapter 2 we looked at the motivated person and the motivating environment in isolation from each other. But this is a somewhat theoretical exercise. The danger that one begins to ask either-or questions presents itself: Is a given motive the result of attributes of the person or of changes in the environment? A similar way of posing the question has led to pointless disputes on the relative importance of heredity and environment. We now know that behavior is always the result of complex interactions between hereditary dispositions and environmental factors, and that the latter have shaped the organism in the past and shape it and affect its behavior in the present. Motives too are always the result of interactions between the person and the environment.

The shift in focus from persons and environments to the interaction between them requires a shift from content theories to process theories (Campbell and Pritchard, 1976). Content theories specify the needs of human beings or the characteristics of the work situation. They are incomplete explanations of motivated behavior. The more complex questions encountered at this point include: How do the person and the environment interact? What are the processes that lead one person to hard work and another to a life of indolence? A new concept enters the picture here: the idea of the person-environment system or the work situation. We encountered this notion in Chapter 1. It refers to the larger and dynamic whole that includes both the worker and the work environment.

The number of different person-environment systems pertaining to work is infinite. Dürrenmatt's Swiss train conductor and the train hurtling toward the center of the earth constitute one; so do the nineteenth-century postman and the inhospitable Sierra Nevada he crossed on skis, and the woman serving coffee in her isolated hut in the Alps. But for purposes of this chapter, consider the following hypothetical and more typical case:

Alfred M. is a middle-aged shoe salesman in a large store. He is divorced and depends on his job to provide the income not only to feed himself, but also to pay child support. Sometimes the owner of the store is on the premises, but usually it is the store manager who supervises the sales personnel. Both owner and manager have made it clear that good work means friendly attentiveness, unobtrusively but constantly exhibited toward anyone who enters the store. This is one of the criteria of good work performance. The other is the number of pairs of shoes sold. When both manager and owner are in the store, Alfred positively beams upon his customers, but when neither is there his thoughts tend to turn to his aching back. He gets along well with his co-workers; when things are slow in the store they animatedly discuss everything from the weather and the latest baseball scores to current family crises.

This chapter seeks to answer the question, "What makes Alfred sell shoes?" It tries to provide a more complete answer than a focus on either the person or the environment can provide. It pursues in more detail the relationships between person and environment outlined in Exhibits 1-1 and 2-1. It does so by looking at Alfred in the light of four major theories of work motivation. These theories are linked to very broad and established accounts of human behavior. They have the potential to provide explanations of depth and scope. What they do not offer is first-order relevance. Deeply rooted and general theories have second-order relevance. Their importance lies in the fact that they provide the underlying relationships and the big picture and that it is from them that operations, techniques, procedures, and so forth of first-order relevance in specific situations can be derived.

In considering these theories it is important to be clear about what it is that they seek to explain. An important distinction must be made here between performance and work behavior other than performance. Some theoretical statements concern the former; others the latter. The distinction is frequently ignored. For example, it is sometimes asserted that a satisfied worker will work hard. A quick analysis that distinguishes between performance and other work behavior reveals that satisfaction may result from rewards that are contingent on work behavior other than performance. An employee may be satisfied with her job and may approach it early in the morning with a jaunty gait and a song on her lips, precisely because it is not mentally taxing, requires no physical effort, and provides ample opportunity to discuss politics and family life in the vicinity of the coffee machine. Performance is thus one thing; absenteeism, turnover (quitting), and tardiness are another. Clearly the latter are, however, often related indirectly to performance. Usually, for example, absent employees cannot perform at a high level.

WEAK INTERACTION THEORY

Electrical engineers distinguish between communication systems that have broad band width and those that have high fidelity. Similarly, scientists distinguish between schemas, models, and theories that make few assumptions and apply in a general way to a wide range of situations, and those that make many and restrictive assumptions and apply with greater accuracy to a more limited domain.

The broad band width schemas, models, and theories are often called "macroscopic," "molar," and "weak"; the high fidelity ones are often called "microscopic," "molecular," and "strong." Early stages of understanding usually involve weak theories; later ones involve strong theories. Ultimately scientists want theories that cover broad domains of phenomena in a specific and accurate way. In motivation we are far from this distant goal, but both weak and strong theories convey useful bits of information on the subject.

Push and Pull Conceptions of Motivation

We have seen that *motivation, power,* and *force* are related words. Particularly the connotation of force raises an issue about motivation that leads from the person and the environment to the interaction between the two. Are motives forces that move us by pushing us or by pulling us? The answer is that they do both, depending on the observer's point of view and on the type of behavior that is under consideration.

Push and Pull Within the Person

We can say that needs push while goals pull. Both generate forces operating from within the person. It does not matter whether the need is a deficit need of interest to the behaviorists or a growth need of the kind that excites Maslow and others. The need to self-actualize impels. It may do so less irresistibly than hunger pangs, but it pushes. Thus both behaviorists and others, such as the proponents of self-actualization, can agree that needs are forces that push. On the other hand, goals pull. Of course, they are also points of contention as far as the behaviorists are concerned.

We can also say that the past pushes while the future pulls. Goals are generally things that lie in the future, a new state of affairs to be arranged by vigorous effort. The past, in contrast, is associated with habits that, once learned, persist into the present (and future), blindly pushing us to behave one way or another. Our goal may be to be healthy, but the past makes us reach out for the offered cigarette. Many of the acquired responses that form the R part of the S-R or stimulus-response connections (called habits) are acquired needs. The child who has been burned by the stove gives the definite impression of being pushed by a fear of it which was acquired in the past.

Needs versus goals and past versus future are thus two contexts of the push-pull dichotomy. Not only are they closely related, but so are what at first sight may appear to be the diametrically opposed poles of each. Needs may determine goals, and what we seek in the future is a function of our past. The person who is high on the need to self-actualize has the goal of becoming a more fully developed person, able to use more of his or her potentials. The person who learned to fear solitude strives to create a future marked by close relationships with others.

Push and Pull Within the Environment

When the focus is on the motivating environment, attention shifts to a different set of constructs: to negative rewards or actual or potential punishments to be escaped from or avoided, and to positive rewards. In general, the former push and the latter pull. But in practice there prevails here a complex set of relationships between what appear on the surface to be opposite poles.

Suppose the environment motivates a worker by displaying a threatening stick. It could, for example, signal "work or go hungry!" In one way the stick is a pushing force, but in another it creates an incentive, the incentive of getting away from the threatened unpleasantness of hunger. Thus an auto worker might hammer rivets with vigor primarily to put food on the table and to avoid facing a family that has eaten nothing but hamburgers for weeks.

Another complication is that there are two quite different kinds of positive rewards. Most positive rewards reduce actual tension; they are carrots. For example, an employer might say to a salesman; "If you sell plenty, you'll have a swimming pool as big as mine." With that promise, goal, or carrot dangling before him, the salesman bursts forth to sell muscle cars to old ladies who only drive to church on Sundays. But some positive rewards are real carrots: for example, the satisfaction obtained by a computer programmer who has finally debugged and successfully run a program after weeks of work. The real carrots are perhaps more clearly forces that pull than rewards that simply reduce pressing needs.

But basically the push-pull dichotomy appears in the context of the environment as something overlapping a great deal with the "carrot versus stick" dichotomy. Anyone who has ever tried to get anyone else to do anything in the absence of intrinsic motivation has learned what every mule driver knows: You can either dangle a carrot in front or threaten with a stick from behind. Sometimes the problem is to choose between these two very different external motivation strategies, although the carrot seems to work far better with humans than does the stick.

One can also approach the push-pull dichotomy from the point of view of the perceived rather than the actual environment. This is the cognitive view of the motivating environment which distinguishes between outcomes with either a positive valence or a negative valence, rather than between objectively existing "carrots" and "sticks." The behavior of a worker has certain expected outcomes. If they are attractive (attracting) outcomes (a larger paycheck, a promotion) they pull and have a positive valence; if they are repelling outcomes (a reprimand, being fired) they push and have negative valence.

The Person Pushes, the Environment Pulls

The person constitutes a set of needs, of general goals, and other dispositions. These dispositions can be regarded as pushing the individual from within. The environment, in the context of motivation, consists mainly of a set of incentives, that is, of potential rewards to be attained or punishments to be avoided. One can argue that whether the incentive is a potential reward or the opportunity to avoid potential or stop actual punishment makes no difference, and that rewards like a sizzling steak and escape from a noxious stimulus like a reprimand both reduce tension and are events that exert a pulling force. Certainly, both of these types of incentives can act as reinforcers, that is, stimuli, conditions, or events that strengthen certain responses.

Before leaving the push-pull dichotomy it may be worthwhile to reiterate the point that, like the person-environment dichotomy, it is a creation of the observer, of the scientist who tries to introduce some order into the messy and confusing real world. Sometimes a dichotomy, like any classification system, fits well. Sometimes it does not. The usefulness of the push-pull dichotomy should not be exaggerated. Drives are pushing forces, but it often takes some external stimulus pattern to elicit them. The smell of a steak can make us hungry. There is really no pull without push, and vice versa. The motivating forces that push and pull thus are not only related, they actually complement each other. We noticed earlier the distinction between drive and motive: The hapless explorer in the desert is driven; thirst pushes him aimlessly around. The thirsty student on campus, familiar with a favorite pub nearby, is motivated. Thirst pushes him, the pub pulls him, and this simultaneous pushing (energy) and pulling (direction) is what we usually mean by motivation.

Multiplicative Relationships

Multiplicative relationships are common in psychological theory. Two have already appeared in Chapter 1. Performance appeared there as the product of worker multplied by work environment. Furthermore, the worker, more specifically the competence he brings to the job, was represented as the product of motivation times ability. For example, if the watchmaker is motivated and has the skills, he is competent to make watches. But if he is tired he will not perform competently, no matter how great his skills and knowledge may be. Neither will the young apprentice who has not yet acquired the necessary skills, no matter how great his enthusiasm.

This assumption that competence is the product of motivation times ability is derived from the learning theory of Hull whose basic postulate is that reaction potential is some function of the product of drive times habit strength. Hull's (1943) theory has the general scope of a weak theory, but it attempts to explain the wide range of behavior to which it addresses itself in terms of specific assumptions and postulates.

In much simplified form, Hull's basic postulate is:

$$\text{Reaction Potential} = \text{Drive} \times \text{Habit Strength}$$

It explains such things as a rat's pressing a bar that causes a food pellet to fall into its cage. The rat does so because it has associated the stimulus *bar* with the response *bar press*. The agent that brought about this stimulus-response connection, or habit, has been the reward: the food pellet which reduced the tensions of hunger in repeated learning trials. But although the rat has acquired this habit of responding to the bar by pressing it, it only presses the bar when it is hungry. Thus only when neither habit strength nor drive is zero is there a reaction potential that causes the animal to respond to the bar.

A multiplicative relationship need not meet all the assumptions of the mathematical operation of multiplication. We consider a relationship to be multiplicative if it reflects the important fact that when something is multiplied by zero, the result must be zero. In this case it would, for example, be unproductive to postulate an additive relationship. Such an assumption would imply that the rat, once it has learned the bar press response, will press its bar whenever it sees it, or whenever it is hungry and regardless of previous learning.

The competence postulate is really Hull's basic postulate translated into more general terms. Motivation is recognizable as drive, ability is a set of habits, and competence is a form of reaction potential.

Reaction potential, competence, and ultimately performance are more general concepts than motivation itself, but motivation too is in turn the product of more specific variables. In their extension of the performance postulate, Campbell and Pritchard (1976) represent it essentially as follows:

$$\text{Work Motivation} = \text{Choice to Expend Energy} \times \text{Choice of Degree of Effort to Expend} \times \text{Choice to Persist}$$

This implies that unless Alfred decides to expend energy *and* to expend a given degree of effort *and* to persist, he will not exhibit *any* motivation to sell shoes.

STRONG INTERACTION THEORY

Here we come to the crux of work motivation, to the more specific explanations of why people act the way they do. There are many different strong interaction theories. The four that will be discussed here have been selected partly because they are widely applied and partly because they exemplify very different approaches. Two of them are so "strong" that they can be formulated mathematically. Their mathematical formulations are presented in Appendix 1, an appendix designed for those who share Whitehead's view that in order to know what a forest is, one should know in detail some of its trees.

Cattell: Sophisticated Need Theory

Raymond B. Cattell (1957) approaches the problem from the point of view of the psychology of personality. He places the emphasis on personality traits or psychological needs. Of particular importance in the context of motivation, of the dynamic aspects of personality, are what Cattell calls "dynamic traits" or "ergs": needs like *security, gregariousness,* and *self-assertion.* One of Cattell's main contributions to the understanding of behavior is his extension of Kurt Lewin's (1935) succinct statement of the proposition that behavior is a function of the person and the environment:

$$\text{Behavior} = f \text{ (Person, Environment)}$$

Just as Campbell and Pritchard extended Vroom's basic postulate by breaking down its global terms, so Cattell and his colleagues essentially broke down the notions of person and environment in Lewin's formula. Cattell's extension treats the person as a set of different traits, that is, dispositions to engage in different behaviors. If we are told that Alfred M. is gregarious, we probably expect more friendly attentiveness from him than if we are told that he is aloof.

So far, we have a person-centered theory. The environment enters the picture in the form of the proposition that specific situations affect or modulate the expression of a trait. A specific situation in Alfred's case is working in the store with the supervisor present. When the supervisor looks over his shoulder, Alfred might curb his gregariousness, in spite of its contribution to desirable friendly attentiveness, because it might seem more important to him to project a professional and restrained image. That does not mean he will fail to exhibit friendly attentiveness. It means that other traits, more approved of by the supervisor than bubbling talkativeness, would be likely to account for it. Alfred's case, as seen within the framework of Cattell's theory, is pursued in more technical fashion in Appendix 1.

Herzberg: Intrinsic and Extrinsic Job Factors

While Cattell's emphasis is on the person, that of Herzberg, Mausner, and Snyderman (1959) is on the work environment. It is an environment-oriented content theory about what Herzberg calls "job factors," that is, broad clusters of aspects of the environment pertaining to such things as the opportunities for obtaining earned rewards and the type of supervision exercised. These job factors overlap with the conditions and agents of the work environment identified in Exhibit 1-1.

Just as Cattell is keenly aware that the person does nothing without an environment, so Herzberg starts with assumptions about needs forming the roots of workers' motivation. These assumptions he adopts from the work of Maslow (1954). There is the assumption that there are two kinds of human needs: basic deficit needs and higher level growth needs. Then there is the somewhat stronger, more specific assumption that higher level needs emerge only after lower level needs have been satisfied.

This brings us to Herzberg's real interest: the work environment consisting of job content and job context. He postulates that there are two kinds of job factors: those that are extrinsic to the work itself and those that are intrinsic in it. Herzberg's extrinsic job factors are company policy and administration, technical supervision, salary, interpersonal relations, and working conditions; his main intrinsic job factors are achievement, recognition, work itself, responsibility, and advancement.

This distinction between intrinsic and extrinsic job factors, what Herzberg calls motivators or satisfiers and hygienes or maintenance factors, is problematic but interesting. It is problematic because the distinction between intrinsic and extrinsic motivation, rewards, and job factors is somewhat fuzzy. Are salary and promotion extrinsic? Is interest elicited by the tasks of a particular job intrinsic? It all depends on the context.

Arie Kruglanski and his colleagues (Kruglanski et al., 1975, 744) point out that while "money constitutes an external object . . . the desire for it may be acutely internal," and that "interest in a task may be internal, yet the task eliciting such interest is certainly external." They also note that money is usually an extrinsic reward, but that it can also inhere in the activity of a person. Kruglanski and his colleagues used money in the context of a coin toss game with children for whom money was an intrinsic part of the game. Without money to be lost or won, it would not have been the same game. They found that money in this situation had the same effects as intrinsic rewards. Shoukry Saleh (1979) notes that advancement or promotion is a job factor that has several dimensions and that the increased challenge offered by a higher level job is probably intrinsic, but the increased salary associated with it is probably extrinsic.

In spite of the fuzziness of the distinction between what is intrinsic and what is extrinsic, Herzberg's distinction between intrinsic and extrinsic job factors is interesting. Herzberg argues that the two types of job factors have quite different effects on the worker and that the absence of hygienes causes dissatisfaction, while the presence of motivators causes satisfaction. He also maintains that work satisfaction and work dissatisfaction are not related to each other, that is, that workers can be both very dissatisfied and very satisfied with a job.

Although the empirical evidence does not support Herzberg's theory in general, he is telling us some things about Alfred M. that are food for thought. He is telling us that Alfred may be dissatisfied with his job if one or more extrinsic job factors are lacking. Providing such job factors might cause him to cease complaining. But, Herzberg argues, such action would not affect his motivation level, it would not make him smile, and it would do nothing for productivity. To make Alfred happy, the management of his shoestore must provide motivators, job factors that are intrinsic in the work. Salary is like an attendance fee; to get Alfred into gear more than extrinsic conditions have to be satisfied.

Vroom: Valence-Instrumentality-Expectancy Theory

We have seen in Chapter 2 that psychologists differ in the degree to which they emphasize drives and the degree to which they emphasize goals. Behaviorist process theories of motivation rely largely on the drive concept; cognitive process theories rely more on goals. It is their focus on what is perceived, rather than on what actually exists, that makes cognitive theories important, and among the cognitive theories of work behavior one of the most influential is that of Vroom (1964).

Vroom's theory rests on two basic notions: the notions of *expectancy* and of *valence*. Expectancies are expressed as probabilities and they reflect how strongly (with what probability) a certain result is expected to occur. Vroom distinguishes between *performance-outcome* expectancies and *effort-performance* expectancies.

Performance-outcome expectancies—Vroom calls them "instrumentalities"—reflect how strongly the worker expects that successful or unsuccesful performance of a task or job will be followed by a given outcome. For example, if Alfred is paid a monthly salary, he expects to be paid at the end of the month whether he is successful or not in selling shoes. Of course, he might also expect to be fired eventually if his performance is unsuccessful.

The performance-outcome expectancies are influenced by at least one personality variable: internal versus external control (Lawler, 1973). Internally controlled persons believe that their efforts will produce the rewards to which successful performance entitles them. Externally controlled persons, on the other hand, believe that what happens to them is largely the result of chance, fate, or luck.

Effort-performance expectancies indicate how strongly a worker expects that effort will lead to a given level of performance. These effort-performance expectancies are not independent of each other. If Alfred distinguishes only two levels of performance, success and failure, and if he thinks that the probability of success is .40, then the value assigned to the probability of failure will have to be .60, since the probability that he will be either successful or unsuccessful must be 1.00.

In general, workers who believe that they can successfully complete a task are more likely to try to do it than workers who do not believe that their efforts will be crowned with success. However, the need to achieve may moderate this straightforward linear relationship: People high on this need are more likely to tackle tasks of moderate difficulty, that is, tasks that are sufficiently difficult to be challenging and allow a sense of achievement, but not difficult enough to lead to disappointing failure. At least one personality trait appears to be linearly linked to effort-performance expectancies. A self-confident person is likely to perceive the probability of success to be higher than one who lacks confidence (Lawler, 1973).

Vroom's second concept critical to understanding the motivational processes operating in the work situation has been touched on above. It is the concept *valence*. If people choose to work hard or to take it easy, it is because they have contemplated the possible outcomes of either course of action. Each outcome has a perceived valence: It is seen to be desirable or undesirable to a greater or lesser extent.

The most common outcome of choosing to work, to make an effort, is that one is paid for it. Money has almost universally high valence because it can procure most satisfactions that are sought at a particular time. The worker who has a strong need to achieve may spend it on tuition for university extension courses, while an insecure person may try to surround him- or herself with secure walls made of money in the bank. Personality differences, in other words, are more related to the reasons for regarding money as desirable and less to whether one regards it as desirable in the first place.

For almost any other outcome, valences will differ widely from person to person. For example, the high achiever will assign a high valence to mastering a difficult task; the status-conscious organization man will labor vigorously for a carpeted office or a pat on the back from the chairman of the board.

From this cognitive perspective we are interested in understanding under what conditions Alfred will choose to make an effort to perform successfully on his job. The details are left for Appendix 1. What is of interest here is that he is likely to make an effort when he expects that making an effort will result in meeting the criteria of high performance in terms of such things as the number of shoes sold, when he expects successful performance to lead to outcomes such as extrinsic assurances from the supervisor that the management is pleased and intrinsic outcomes such as pride in his work, and when he perceives these outcomes to have high positive valences. He is not likely to make an effort when performance standards are so high that he does not expect to attain them anyway, when it is not clear that management is paying attention and will remember to provide rewarding outcomes, and when certain outcomes are expected but do not seem worthwhile.

Skinner: Reinforcement Theory

A fourth way of trying to understand the motivated behavior of Alfred M. is in terms of reinforcement theory. We have encountered Skinner, its source, before and can expect it to lay heavy emphasis on the environment. However, like any serious motivation theory it must address itself to the interaction between person and environment.

Skinner defines reinforcers as stimuli that increase the probability of the response learned or to be learned. Others define reinforcers as stimuli that change (i.e., increase or decrease) the probability of the response. The latter school of thought is the mainstream school and we will return to it in the chapters on ability. Mainstream thinking differs from that of Skinner in that it assumes that punishment—the presentation of negative reinforcers like a pink slip, a fine, or a reprimand—decreases the probability of responses to be unlearned. Skinner does not believe that any reinforcers, positive or negative, reduce the probability of a response.

Skinner would be interested in teaching Alfred to be more productive. This would involve analysis of his work behavior and identification of target behaviors that should be strengthened. For example, Alfred might be reinforced with a small bonus for each day during which he approaches the next customer within five seconds of being free.

A number of points are suggested by this look at Alfred in the context of a shoestore in which the principles of reinforcement theory are known and applied.

First, there is a program, a set of operations that are executed to affect his level of motivation. The intent is to make him more productive, to raise his performance level perhaps not only in terms of the speed with which he approaches the next customer, but also in terms of other criteria such as the number of shoes sold per day or the number of customers approached with friendly attentiveness. Whatever the responses underlying his higher level of performance may be, they are reinforced and strengthened. They may be motivational responses, such as a positive attitude toward customers, or they may be new skills. In this chapter it is the former that we have in mind; the latter are more relevant in the chapters on ability.

Second, the reinforcer must be contingent on the behavior to be learned, acquired, or strengthened. Skinner points out that in the workplace rewards are usually not contingent on desired behavior. Does the worker perform to obtain the paycheck at the end of the week? No, says Skinner; that's too far away to cause the worker to work harder on Monday. Not only is the interval between response and reinforcement long, the reinforcer is presented regardless of whether performance was high or low during the week. Of course, if an ultimatum was issued to the worker, the paycheck would be on the line and contingent on the work. Typically, however, one works to avoid surly glances from the boss, threats of dismissal, and other negative reinforcers.

Skinnerians also maintain that the reinforcer must be timed effectively. Skinner initially worked with rats and pigeons and he observed that continuous reinforcement, a schedule that calls for reinforcing every correct response (i.e., every response learned or to be learned), led to rapid acquisition of the response. But when the reinforcers were withdrawn, there was also rapid extinction of the response. On the other hand, under a partial or intermittent reinforcement schedule, say one that called for reinforcement after random numbers of correct responses (e.g., after responses 4, 10, 19, 21, and so forth), both acquisition and extinction were slow.

The research suggests that in the case of human workers, reinforcement schedules interact with expectations and perceptions. This is one case in which generalizations from animals to humans may be unwarranted. Alfred may not perceive intermittent reinforcement as intermittent at all (Landy, 1985, 362). Human beings have a tendency to interpret what goes on around them in complex ways.

Judiciously identifying responses to be reinforced and making his reinforcers contingent on them, Skinner was able to perform near-miracles of behavior shaping. He was able to teach pigeons to play baseball; clinical psychologists were able to teach mute psychiatric patients to speak. Shaping involves waiting until a response is emitted that the shaper wishes to encourage because it is a little closer to the desired behavior than any of the other responses made by the subject. For example, the mute patient may be reinforced for clearing his throat. If the reinforcer is effective, the patient may clear his throat more frequently. At a certain point, the shaper decides to reinforce only responses that are closer to speaking: clearing of the throat accompanied by speech-like sounds. Eventually, only speech itself may be reinforced.

Skinner's contribution to motivation theory is sometimes called a technology rather than a theory (Landy, 1985). Skinner himself proudly claimed to deal in empirical relationships rather than theories, and indeed the relationships between behavior and reinforcers that he established are powerful. Nevertheless, reinforcement theory is of interest in a chapter on theories of work motivation striving to promote understanding characterized by depth and scope. While Skinner's postulates about reinforcement, contingency, and timing may not constitute a theory, the learning theory in which they are embedded certainly offers depth in the form of links to basic constructs underlying behavior and scope in the form of links to a wide range of behavior.

4.

Optimizing Work Motivation

The question now arises whether a better understanding of motivation provided by theories like those of Cattell, Herzberg, Vroom, and Skinner can be applied to increase performance and work satisfaction. The proof of the usefulness of a theory is how well it fits the situations to which it is meant to apply and the extent to which it permits prediction and control in these situations. Do our motivation theories help us understand and cope with bureaucratic lethargy, strikes in the public service, sabotage, vandalism, and high absenteeism rates?

Our theories may not be *immediately* useful. They have second-order rather than first-order relevance. They direct attention to what is common in many work situations and provide an understanding of broad motivational processes. They do not tell us what to do in particular situations. However, we can often derive from them insights and procedures that have first-order relevance in the store, in the plant, and in the office. The concern shifts here from depth and scope, from theoretical understanding of the whole range of motivated behavior, to applications of specific knowledge in specific situations.

The bookshelves and publishers' catalogues are full of how-to books promising fantastic results in infinitesimally short periods of time. That is not what this chapter is about. It is about a number of conclusions that can serve to guide attempts to optimize work motivation.

PROMOTING CONGRUENCE OF NEEDS AND REWARDS

We have seen that if there are needs, and if the environment offers rewards that can satisfy them, there is likely to be willingness to work for these rewards. Congruence of needs and rewards appears to be a basic requirement if people are to work, and that requirement emerges clearly whether the approach to motivation is push-oriented or pull-oriented, behaviorist or cognitive.

Cattell's theory provides a useful framework for looking at the degree of congruence between needs and potential rewards. While it places the emphasis on the traits (personality characteristics) of the worker, it shows how these traits differ in relevance to particular behaviors demanded by the situation and in the degree to which they are elicited by the situation. In Alfred M.'s case, we saw that gregariousness was a factor in determining the desired behavior of friendly attentiveness which was elicited more strongly when the supervisor was away than when he was in the store.

From the practical point of view, Cattell's most important contribution consists of his personality tests, in particular the Sixteen Personality Factor Questionnaire (16PF; Cattell, Eber, and Tatsuoka, 1970). Promoting congruence of needs and potential rewards requires a knowledge of what needs the worker is bringing to the job. Since rewards are things that satisfy needs, knowing what the worker's needs are allows one to identify or arrange appropriate rewards.

The 16PF was developed by correlating many potentially useful self-report items. These items were one-sentence statements with which the respondents were asked to agree or disagree. The responses obtained from many respondents were subjected to factor analysis, a procedure that reveals a small number of broad and underlying dimensions (the factors) that account for the correlations between many variables or items. The results of Cattell's analyses are 16 basic personality factors such as "outgoing versus reserved" and a number of items that measure each factor. For example, if the subject responds in the "outgoing" direction to many items measuring the "outgoing versus reserved" factor, a high score will be obtained.

Knowing something about the needs of the worker allows one to either fit him or her to an available job by making sure that the rewards it offers meet his or her needs, or to fit the job to him or her by changing it in some way. Chapter 10 looks at this process of matching people and jobs from a broader point of view which includes not only motivation but also the second category of personal characteristics determining performance: the person's abilities, skills, and knowledge.

RELYING ON INTRINSIC MOTIVATION

A second conclusion that a better understanding of motivation probably permits one to draw is that the best workers are the intrinsically motivated ones. This is a conclusion that is suggested primarily by the work of Herzberg.

As noted earlier, the distinction between things intrinsic and extrinsic can be fuzzy. According to Webster's *Third New International Dictionary*, intrinsic means "belonging to the inmost constitution or essential nature of a thing." Extrinsic is used to refer to something that does not belong to or is not a property of something. It follows that all needs, since they reside in the person, are intrinsic in the person, and that all environmental factors, since they reside in the environment, are extrinsic to the person. More generally, it follows that the terms intrinsic and extrinsic are useless by themselves. To make them meaningful one must specify what it is that is supposed to be intrinsic or extrinsic. Is it a reward, a broad environmental factor, a need or motive, or motivation in general? Furthermore, one must specify exactly *in* what the reward, environmental factor, or motive is intrinsic or *to* what it is extrinsic.

Exhibit 1-1 reflects the dichotomy of intrinsic and extrinsic job dimensions, job factors, or aspects of the work situation. Intrinsic conditions are generally intrinsic in the work; the one intrinsic agent—the self—is intrinsic in the person. Both extrinsic conditions and extrinsic agents are extrinsic to both work and to the person.

Herzberg's central distinction is between job factors intrinsic in the work and those extrinsic to it. Those that are intrinsic in the work are always associated with it: The work may be intrinsically challenging or it may intrinsically offer opportunities to learn new skills and assume new responsibility. These job factors intrinsic in the work tend to provide rewards that satisfy Maslow's higher level needs, for example, the needs to achieve, to grow, to assume responsibility. Presumably because rewards intrinsic in work satisfy them, these needs are often thought of as constituting intrinsic motivation.

Intrinsic motivation in this sense is stronger, more reliable, and more useful than extrinsic motivation. It is relevant to the task at hand; that is, it involves rewards that can only be obtained by doing the work (which are invariably contingent on doing the work). This makes them strong reinforcers of the behavior that produces them. A sense of accomplishment requires doing a challenging job. Money, on the other hand, can be obtained from rich uncles or from appropriate governmental agencies.

The rewards intrinsic in work are "real carrots," that is, rewards that are positive and that attract us. Herzberg argues that they are offered by his motivators, the job factors intrinsic in the work. They must be differentiated clearly from the rewards extrinsic to the work—either negative rewards consisting of avoidance or escape from some deliberately threatened punishment or apparent carrots that permit us to avoid or escape from an unpleasant condition such as hunger or poverty.

According to Herzberg, the basic motive for working is to avoid dissatisfaction, tension, or pain. This means that extrinsic rewards can be powerful agents in manipulating behavior. They built the pyramids and the Great Wall of China. It is clear, however, that they do not instill work satisfaction and sustained interest in doing the work.

Once extrinsic rewards have satisfied basic needs, workers can strive for the real carrots intrinsic in the work they do. The computer scientist who burns the midnight oil until the problem is solved is probably motivated by the real carrot of attaining satisfaction rather than by the opportunity to avoid dissatisfaction.

Unfortunately, not all jobs are like that of the computer programmer. Not all jobs entail variety and responsibility, an opportunity to complete one's task and to admire one's handiwork. One of the biggest challenges to industrial and organizational psychology is to show that many jobs can be redesigned so that they offer real carrots.

SETTING GOALS

As the name of this approach to optimizing work motivation suggests, it is a cognitive one. It assumes that goals have important effects on performance, and some of its roots can be traced to Vroom's work and to valence-instrumentality-expectancy theory.

The Central Role of Goals

Most people have experienced the so-called Zeigarnik effect. They have set themselves a goal and they find it difficult to stop because they have not yet attained it. Maybe the goal is to reassemble a bicycle; maybe it is to finish a report. Landy (1985, 337, 342) cites a number of authors who have pointed out that goals provide "traction" rather than "distraction" (Baldamus, 1952), that "intentional behavior . . . tends to keep going until it reaches completion" (Ryan, 1970), and that goals quite generally protect people from excessive emotions and fantasies (Feather and Bond, 1983). Landy also notes that the "humble 'things to do' list . . . may be the single most effective way of blunting depression and lethargy."

One of the most important functions of goals is that they facilitate feedback. They provide points of reference with which one's performance or that of others can be compared. Feedback informs us where we stand, how our performance level stacks up. In addition, it can also be a reinforcer. It may be reinforcing because it reduces uncertainty or provides, if the goals are attained or exceeded, downright satisfaction.

Goal Acceptance and Goal Commitment

Given this central role of goals, one is inclined to look to Vroom and his camp for a better understanding of the process involved in setting goals. Vroom basically asks three questions (see Landy, 1985, 328): (1) Will increased effort make it more likely that performance will be more successful? (2) What rewards will result from more successful performance? (3) Are these rewards worthwhile?

The first of these questions concerns effort-performance expectancies, the second concerns the second-order valence of performance levels, and the third concerns first-order valences of specific outcomes. If the answer to all three questions is *yes*, the worker is likely to choose the option of making a greater effort. In the present context, making a greater effort means setting a more difficult goal for oneself.

This helps to understand the process by which goals are set. There is, however, more to this process. Goal setting has two aspects which are distinct and affected by different variables. These two aspects have been differentiated and analysed by Locke and his colleagues (Locke et al., 1981).

The first aspect of goal setting is goal acceptance. There are some indications that workers are more likely to accept goals if they participated in their formulation. In some countries, like Sweden, the concept of industrial democracy is anchored in legislation and the worker has considerable input in formulating the goals that will be pursued. In other contexts, goals are assigned. This is more typical of the United States in which management assigns goals to workers who relinquish any interest in the process of goal setting in return for ample compensation and fringe benefits.

The second aspect of goal setting is goal commitment. Here extrinsic factors, such as money, appear to play a role. Once a goal has been accepted, money can increase the valence of attaining it and hence increase the worker's commitment to it. In other words, money may affect the amount of energy workers are willing to expend to attain goals they have accepted.

Goal commitment is also affected by the nature of the goal. In particular, difficult and specific goals lead to greater expenditure of energy than easy and vague goals. Since valence-instrumentality-expectancy theory postulates that effort-performance expectancy drops as goal difficulty rises, it seems to contradict goal setting theory and to predict greater expenditure of energy if the goals are easy. However, the lowered effort-performance expectancy is typically more than counterbalanced by the higher valence of more challenging goals (Matsui, Okada, and Mizuguchi, 1981).

The greater effectiveness of specific goals is probably due to their greater ability to provide traction, reduce distraction, and impose structure. In addition, when goals are specific, feedback can be direct and unambiguous.

MAKING REWARDS CONTINGENT ON PRODUCTIVE BEHAVIOR

Contingency on the Level of Society

The importance of the degree to which both the work organization and the society link positive and negative rewards to performance can hardly be overestimated. In the United States this link survives, and there is still an ideological commitment to free enterprise in many circles. Children are encouraged to earn money on sticky August days by selling peculiar-looking concoctions they are pleased to call lemonade. Junior Achievement clubs flourish from coast to coast. The captains of industry and the politicians sing the praise of individual initiative. While government regulations, legal constraints, and the near-monopolistic power of some large corporations inhibit it, free enterprise still holds the promise of wealth for those willing to work and to take risks. This promise accounts in large part for the fact that the American economy is infinitely more productive than that of the Soviet Union.

One example of a lack of rewards contingent on performance in the Soviet Union concerns socialist service in restaurants. Vodka and caviar may be served quickly if the waiters are paid a bonus when the restaurant sales exceed certain norms. But meals, pushing the sales figure up more slowly and requiring more work, are another matter. One traveler reports: "I once asked for [chicken trepang]. 'You won't eat it,' the waiter said. 'Why not?' I asked. 'It's disgusting,' he answered. He was right" (Binyon, 1978).

In the United States, too, the link between work done and rewards obtained is becoming more tenous. That at least partly explains why litter accumulates under the beds in the best of hotels; why signs like "no information here," "closed," "exact change only," "no change without a purchase," and "next wicket" abound; why the old maxim "the customer is always right" has gone the way of the dinosaur.

Contingency on the Level of the Worker

A knowledge of the worker's needs allows one to identify effective rewards that work for the particular person. Matters need not stop there. Reinforcement theory suggests that these rewards can be used to change, improve, and manipulate the worker's behavior. This raises a ticklish issue: Is it ethical to manipulate behavior? One's answer may depend on whether the manipulating is done above board—whether clear agreements are reached between workers and management about which behaviors will lead to which rewards.

One of the attractive aspects of reinforcement theory is that it is simple and can be translated directly into effective operations that enhance performance, presumably by increasing work motivation. Operant conditioning, the technique derived from the reinforcement theory of Skinner, has been applied in many settings ranging from psychiatric institutions to schools.

The setting of interest here is the work organization. One example of an application of reinforcement theory is that reported by Luthans, Paul, and

Baker (1981). Among other things, these investigators used *time off* as a reinforcer of productive selling, stocking, and attendance behavior in a department store. For example, clerks who were absent from their work station 10 percent of the time or less during a one-week period received one hour of paid time off.

The contingent reinforcement proved to be effective, and even when the reinforcers were no longer available, the frequency of the desired behaviors remained higher than it had been before the experimental treatment. In other words, contingent rewards were effective and the reinforcement schedule produced behavior resistant to extinction. Consistent with the discussion of reinforcement theory in the previous chapter and in the context of other studies, this suggests that contingency is important and that the reinforcement schedule makes little difference in this type of situation. Continuous reinforcement seems to produce responses as resistant to extinction as does intermittent reinforcement.

The notion of contingent reinforcement is related to the dichotomy of intrinsic and extrinsic rewards. In general, satisfaction leads to better performance only if it is contingent on performance. The satisfaction that depends on rewards intrinsic in doing the work is by definition contingent on it. The satisfaction of having built a cottage with one's own hands, having sculpted a craggy face, or having written a lucid memorandum cannot be attained without doing the work.

Satisfaction that depends on extrinsic rewards, on the other hand, may or may not be contingent on performance. In a free-enterprise economy they usually are. That does not mean that there are no forces at work trying to separate them from performance in many contexts. It often seems that incompetence in the civil service is barely detectable in the slow and inexorable shuffling of documents that keeps it busy. There are unions that reject merit-based compensation and that vigorously seek to apply the Iron Law of Seniority when it comes to promotions and layoffs. There are managers who tend to punish workers for not performing rather than to reward them for performing.

Even when extrinsic rewards are contingent on performance, they may not work. Workers are more than the machines the orthodox behaviorists perceive them to be. Their perceptions matter. They resent being treated like mules pushed by stick-wielding drivers behind them and pulled by carrots dangled in front of them. Also, when external rewards are arranged to be contingent on the work done, intrinsic motivation sometimes decreases because workers feel increasingly that what they do depends on external factors (Deci, 1975) and because they become more tempted to do only those things that lead to the external rewards. For example, if compensation is based on quantity produced, quality is likely to suffer. Thus there may be many widgets, but the care with which they are assembled and packed may not be of amazing intensity.

The least effective way to generate work motivation is to rely on extrinsic rewards that are not contingent on performance. Extrinsic rewards contingent on performance are likely to be more effective, although they can reduce intrinsic motivation and direct the attention of employees exclusively to those facets of the work that most clearly pay off. The best workers are intrinsically motivated. They want those rewards that can only be obtained by doing their jobs well. These rewards are very effective because they are intrinsically contingent.

The satisfaction of a job well done, the answers provided by innovative approaches to the job, the broadened horizons or awareness obtained by not only doing the job but also finding out what the best ways of doing it are—all of these are powerful intrinsically contingent rewards. The intrinsic motivation they satisfy cannot be produced by clever manipulation. It is something the worker brings to the job and it depends on child-rearing practices and the education system. Parents and teachers are thus crucial agents in determining the vigor with which Americans approach work.

More generally, the various approaches to motivation considered here suggest that it is not a simple question of blaming a lazy populace, or monotonous jobs, or low drive levels (weak pushes) in a satiated and affluent society, or a lack of goals (weak pulls) offered by profit-hungry managers. A host of different factors interact in the system we call "the work situation." All of them have to be considered by both workers and employers if there are to be more heroes in the battle for a higher quality of life like the Sierra Nevada postman.

PART II.

ABILITY

5.

The Able Worker and the Enabling Environment

The man in the department store is on the verge of buying the electric train set. It is well designed and complete, ready to be assembled and to provide thrills to both father and son. A few more questions occur to him: How long has the store carried the item? How long has it carried other items from the same manufacturer? Who provides repair services? Will additional parts be available to extend the set?

The salesgirl becomes apologetic. She does not know. She is sorry. Gradually she also becomes a little uncomfortable and a little irritated. The customer asks if the manager might be able to provide the information. She hesitates. The manager is not available. The assistant manager is eventually located. He talks soothingly. He exudes confidence. He smiles a lot. The store stands behind its products. There is no problem. The customer decides to think it over and leaves the store.

Another customer is looking at electric razors. The sales clerk is a woman in her early thirties. She demonstrates the different makes and models. She unscrews the housing of one to show how simple and hence robust it is. She points out disadvantages and advantages. Her answers to questions are factual and informative.

The very young salesgirl in the first store recently quit high school. She had received a few tips on customer relations and on handling the cash register. The store is not interested in training her carefully because she might quit to get married, to finish high school, to go to college, or to work in another store. Her assistant manager takes business courses at the university and he learned to be interested in sales, not in the products sold.

The sales clerk of the second store, on the other hand, has gone to primary and secondary schools that insisted on proficiency in the basics. The schools had taught her to read, write, and handle numbers. They prepared her for a carefully regulated three-year apprenticeship consisting of work under the supervision of experienced personnel, in her case the owner of a small store. During her apprenticeship she studied subjects like commercial law, correspondence, and accounting at the local vocational school for one and a half days each week. The store she now works for has to compete with small specialty stores, and as a result its management is concerned not just with large-scale merchandising, but also with giving the demanding customers exactly what they want.

The different experiences of our two customers illustrate the point that motivation is not enough. Workers must not only want to do their job, they must also be able to do it. As noted in Chapter 1, competence is the product of motivation and ability. To satisfy clients, a sales clerk must exhibit both.

Our two sales clerks are not hypothetical cases. The first worked in Detroit. She was enthusiastic and friendly enough, but because she did not know anything, she did not sell the train or satisfy the customer. The second worked for a department store in Switzerland. She was the product of the German and Swiss *dual system* of training obtained simultaneously in school and on the job. Her training lasted three years, and this explains why she not only was motivated, but also had the required skills, broader abilities, and knowledge that made her competent.

Like motivation, ability can be approached by looking at the person, then the environment, and finally the interaction between the two. But in the context of ability, the stage of development of a person is of critical importance since aptitudes change over time in a way that is more systematic and predictable than changes in motivation. Ability is initially largely a function of biological aptitudes or capacities. Later, for example at the point at which the young adult leaves school to join the workforce, ability is largely a function of the interaction between the intial biological aptitudes and the formal education system. In still later stages, it is also determined by experiences and learning on the job. As Exhibit 2-1 suggests, at these different stages of development both the person and the environment assume different forms.

THE ABLE WORKER

The worker, employee, manager, entrepreneur—the working individual—brings to the job certain aptitudes, abilities, and skills. These three terms have been defined differently by psychologists, but they all belong to the realm that Lee J. Cronbach (1984) referred to as that of "maximum performance," and they are different from the majority of personality constructs that belong to Cronbach's realm of "typical performance."

In the realm of maximum performance we are interested in what a person *can* do under optimal conditions, given high motivation level and excellent training. In the realm of typical performance what matters is what a person is *likely* to do. Such typical performance is based on personality constructs other than aptitudes, on constructs like personality traits, interests, and values.

One way to differentiate among the three maximum performance constructs of aptitude, ability, and skill is to distinguish between capacities or potentials on one hand and what the person can actually do on the other. The former are largely biological and given; the latter are capacities transformed into demonstrable proficiency or achievement. Aptitudes are thought of as capacities that do not reveal themselves in effective behavior unless education or training have translated them into relatively broad abilities or relatively specific skills.

General Abilities and Computer Literacy

General abilities will be defined here as broad abilities that are important in coping with the world in general. They are the fundamental abilities, the substrate on which vocational abilities and job-specific skills can develop. They are abilities because they are measurable, but they come closest to the as-yet-undeveloped aptitudes. They primarily fall into the cognitive domain; they pertain to the "awareness and understanding of the . . . environment" (Dunnette, 1976, 483). Psychologists sometimes refer to them as "mental abilities" and as "intelligence."

There is agreement that the most important of these general abilities include verbal comprehension (the ability to understand spoken or written material), word fluency (the ability to think of synonyms, antonyms, and so forth), numerical ability (the ability to solve mathematical problems), spatial ability (the ability to visualize things, to orient oneself in the presence of misleading cues), memory, perceptual speed (the ability to see similarities and differences in visual configurations), and inductive reasoning (the ability to discover rules, principles, and patterns). (See Dunnette, 1976, 478.)

It seems apparent that all of these general abilities will help make life easier for anyone who has a job that is not purely routine. Particularly the abilities to juggle words and numbers appear to be tools essential to straight thinking and to communication. Words and numbers enable people to understand what goes on around them, to read the newspapers, to read instructions on how to use a new machine, to complete tax returns and add up invoices. They make it possible to learn on one's own and to extend one's horizon on the job, in vocational schools, and in the colleges and universities. They are not only the foundation of occupational skills later developed through vocational or professional training and on the job, they also underlie the very creativity, imagination, and originality that the schools of the 1960s wanted to achieve directly and without "wasting time" on what they considered to be "pedestrian" basic skills.

Given the changing work environment, the general abilities are particularly relevant. They are required of those who work with computers. Literacy and numeracy both are foundations of what is rather loosely called "computer literacy." This is true regardless of whether a person's work with computers involves merely using them as tools, as in word processing, whether it involves programming computers using high level languages like BASIC or FORTRAN, whether it requires the use of less user-friendly machine language because the higher level languages available do not meet particular needs, or whether it involves computer design, computer repairs, or systems analysis.

It is true that some people see concern about computer literacy as a fad. Peter Wagschal (1978), for example, recounts how he wondered whether his three-year-old son should suffer the agonies of learning the three Rs if, by the time he is 18, computers will respond to voice commands and will program each other. There is talk of artificial intelligence made possible by new computer architectures that allow parallel, rather than the present sequential, processing. The possibility of a return to pictographic rather than alphabetic scripts has also been raised because they could permit more direct communication between computers and human operators. The problem of large numbers of characters is one computers are uniquely able to handle and some of the difficulties inherent in communication could thus be shifted from the human operator to the computer (Thompson, 1979). It has been said that computers have become user-friendly, that they will become very, very friendly, and that ultimately they will become downright "congenial interfaces" (Baker, 1983).

Others see computer literacy as a desirable but not necessary characteristic of most people in the future. Joseph Weizenbaum (e.g., Aeppel, 1983) of the Massachusetts Institute of Technology argues that what most people will need is "information machine savvy"—an ability to use automatic bank tellers and the knowledge that computer billing errors can be corrected no matter how often some customer relations person says, "We can't change it because it is in the computer."

But the most common view, and the one most likely to reflect the real situation in the immediate future, is that computer literacy will be required of all those involved in nonroutine jobs. Computer literacy and employability are likely to go hand in hand, and employees who know how to program and to patch (to change individual bytes of information to tailor available programs to particular needs) are likely to be more useful than employees who give up as soon as a computer system does not allow them to do the job at hand with a few memorized steps. (See Cetron, 1983.)

Vocational Abilities

Vocational abilities differ from general abilities in that they are always directly relevant to work of some kind. Marvin Dunnette distinguishes between two categories of vocational abilities: cognitive and motor. Cognitive abilities pertain to "awareness and understanding of the elements of our environment" (Dunnette, 1976, 483). They can be either general or vocational. For example, solving mathematics problems reflects general cognitive abilities, while repairing an engine by visualizing the problem, noting relationships, and recognizing basic physical principles involved reflects a vocational ability, in particular mechanical ability.

Motor abilities pertain to "the physical manipulation of objects in the environment" (Dunnette, 1976, 483). The mechanic, for example, must not only understand how the machine works, but must also have a certain dexterity to take it apart and put it together again.

While these vocational abilities are clearly linked to the work process, they are still rather broad. It is job-specific abilities or skills that ultimately matter. These again can be cognitive or motor, and at this level of specificity a third category, interpersonal skills, emerges. Cognitive skills of managers can be assessed in management assessment centers by means of simulated managerial work involving an in-basket full of problematic missives that must be dealt with. The motor skills of a forklift operator can be measured by means of work performance samples obtained in a mock-up of a warehouse, or a real warehouse, in which the worker must move goods. An interesting example of developing and assessing interpersonal skills comes from Japan: Workers are trained to bow and smile in front of an elaborate machine showing a silhouette of a body in three different bowing positions. With a mirror the trainees can verify the correctness of their position (Woronoff, 1983).

There is a trend toward focusing on job-specific skills, and toward the work performance samples and simulations that can be used to assess them. It may well be that job-specific measures are simply better predictors of actual job performance in specific settings than are tests of broader vocational abilities, let alone tests of general abilities. Concern about equal rights and equal opportunity makes it mandatory that employers use measures in personnel selection that are demonstrably useful in making predictions about future job performance. Gone are the days in which an applicant for the job of custodian could be rejected automatically for scoring low on a test of general verbal ability.

THE ENABLING ENVIRONMENT

Parallel to the general abilities and to the vocational abilities and skills of the preceding section, there are two different enabling environments: the environment of general education and that of vocational training. The first of these is typically an institutional environment; the second ranges from formal programs in universities to informal workshops and quick on-the-job training sessions in offices and plants.

General Education

The main environments of general education are the general education and college preparatory programs of high schools, the college transfer programs and terminal general education programs of the community colleges, and most of the programs of the four-year colleges and of the universities. These environments are meant to encourage educational activities (i.e., activities that meet education philosopher Richard Peters' [1965] three criteria of being valuable in themselves, of being cared about by the learner, and of deepening understanding and broadening the range of awareness).

Reading one of Plato's Dialogues is an educational activity for those who do it voluntarily. They do it as an end in itself, not because it will make them better car salesmen. They must care about reading and interpreting the material since there is no extrinsic motivation to compel them to engage in this activity in the first place. It will extend their awareness of problems in broad realms like ethics and politics.

This raises an interesting question: Is general education not primarily concerned with the three Rs, with basic skills in handling words and numbers? If so, are these activities really educational in Peters' sense?

Most of the initial schooling is, or should be, spent in learning how to read, write, and compute. Such learning does not meet Peters' three criteria. Mastering the three Rs is a function of training rather than education, of structured curricula with specific objectives that are determined by teachers rather than learners. The reason the three Rs are a central concern of general education programs is not that they are educational, but that without them no educational activities can take place.

The term *educational institution* is really a self-contradiction. An institution implies specific objectives and standard procedures, that is, training. Education, on the other hand, is a personal activity that takes place all the time and in the most unstructured environments. Thus, in practice, much of general education is actually structured training whose aim is to provide the tools that make education possible.

Vocational Training

While institutionalized education is sometimes taken for something other than training, there is no doubt about vocational training. It clearly is not education because it does not seek to meet Peters' criterion of cognitive breadth, of broadening the learner's awareness and understanding of the environment and him- or herself. It is governed by practical concerns and seeks to attain them in a direct, hence explicitly structured way. Specific goals are usually set and step-by-step programs to attain them are devised.

Good training programs try to meet the other two of the criteria of educational activities. To some degree they can be ends in themselves that contribute to the development of the learner—for example, by strengthening a sense of discipline and precision—and they can generate great interest and care on the part of the learner.

Vocational training can begin any time after primary school, once the three Rs have more or less been mastered. At that point a decision has to be made: Will the focus of future educational activity be on general "education" or on vocational training?

On the secondary school level, a student can enroll in vocational programs offered by comprehensive high schools or in separate vocational schools. Such early choice of the vocational route is generally associated with low socioeconomic status. The poor are more likely to be faced with demands to acquire salable skills quickly and start to help put food on the table. There are suggestions, however, that performance levels in these programs are higher than those in the general education programs at the secondary level. In fact, while the college preparatory programs of the high schools confer the highest status, it is not the vocational programs that offer the lowest status. Rather, it is the general education programs that are said to be those selected by "rejects" (Evans and Herr, 1978, 69)

In the postsecondary schools the range of options increases dramatically. The two-year community colleges offer, besides college transfer programs and terminal general education programs, vocational programs in such areas as nursing, technology, office work, and commercial occupations. Some of these colleges have a tendency to pursue activities perceived to have high status: the college transfer programs and technology programs that really stress physics and mathematics rather than the demands of the jobs their trainees will hold. Here, as in the high schools, vocational training is not regarded with universal respect.

At the postsecondary level there are also technical institutes and four-year colleges. The latter offer programs in areas such as technology whose graduates function at a level between those of graduates of the community colleges and those of the universities. Even the universities are not averse to vocational training; after all, many of them were land grant universities with the very practical objective of training farmers to produce better crops.

Proprietary vocational schools also can play a useful role. They are run for profit, and to benefit from their services one has to be able to afford their fee. However, being profit-oriented they will, if they are good schools, adapt quickly to the marketplace and offer programs in fields in which trained people are required. In the past they have concentrated on occupations like hotel management, truck driving, and hair styling; more recently there has been an emphasis on data processing. Not all of these schools are good; some are fly-by-night operations promising much and delivering little help in finding a job after the training is completed.

Most vocational training is more directly linked to the workplace, however, than to the schools. Many schools have vocational cooperative programs supervised by coordinators who locate employers able to offer part-time employment related to the student's work in school. These supervisors typically teach the courses constituting the school's contribution to the program. The part-time student of a high school, college, or university thus is at the same time a part-time employee of a cooperating firm; classroom instruction is supplemented by on-the-job training.

Some programs are offered entirely within the world of work. Employer training programs may be offered through the training departments of large corporations, company-owned schools, management assessment centers, apprenticeship programs, and outside trainers and consultants. They range from elaborate management training to quick on-the-job training of custodians and parcel wrappers. Various unions run their own programs. In general the unions are more interested than the employers in thorough training and in portable qualifications.

The training of apprentices falls into a separate category. It may be largely handled by an employer or by a union. But one must sharply distinguish here between registered and unregistered apprenticeships. The latter can be informal; the former are typically supervised jointly by employers, unions, and governments. They are more likely to result in certified and hence portable qualifications.

Finally there are vocational training programs offered by the armed services; by vendors of the new electronic office equipment, computers, and telecommunications devices; by professional and trade organizations seeking to update the qualifications of their members; and by a variety of agencies ranging from the YMCA to schools and universities in the form of adult education and extension courses for students who did not complete high school or are hard to reach. Then there are special courses, offered by this same range of institutions, designed for the disabled and other special groups and frequently funded under federal programs.

The possibilities are there. The question that arises is: Are they being used to full advantage?

In general, the answer seems to be "no." In education, there is a tendency to look down on vocational training. The average American is supposed to go to college. In business, there is a tendency to invest as little in the training of human resources as possible. Compared with Japanese and German employers, American corporations spend small amounts on the training of their workers. It is true that management training is pursued quite vigorously, but nonmanagement employees, constituting a large majority, are trained as rapidly as possible on the assumption that an expensively and well-trained worker, say a salesperson who actually understands the product being sold, would be able to command a higher salary or get another job. Often large corporations hire workers trained by smaller firms. Since the costs of training do not immediately affect productivity, impatient managers prefer to go the route of simplifying jobs rather than training workers to handle more complex and satisfying jobs more competently. The question of whether Americans are undertrained is a troublesome one which will come up again in the context of matching people and jobs on the macro level of the national workforce.

6.

Interaction Between Able Worker and Enabling Environment

As in the case of motivation, we proceed from the simplifying and useful fiction that the person and the environment can be treated as separate entities to the complex interaction between the two that prevails in reality. But while there are a number of strong theories of motivation, there is less theory on the interaction of worker and training environments.

To the extent that there is a theoretical orientation, it is focused on the individual person engaged in the process of learning. The individual is a relatively small system. John Hinrichs (1976) calls it a "skill acquisition system" and contrasts it with two larger systems: the training department of a work organization and the work organization itself. At the level of the individual, the resolution level is high; on this micro or molecular level we see very specific processes close up. It is these circumscribed processes that are the focus of learning theory.

Most practical concerns about training pertain to the level of the training department, programs, or schools. On this macro or molar level the resolution is lower; the processes looked at cover a wider scope and are of more immediately practical concern. Training on this macro level is what primarily interests the business world and most educators, because it is here that there are visible payoffs in terms of changed and improved performance.

The orientation of this book, of course, is that theory and applications are *both* important—that theory has second-order relevance because it allows us in the long run to derive solutions, programs, and techniques that have first-order relevance in day-to-day efforts to cope with concrete problems. In this context, the concrete problems pertain to training people so their skills, abilities, and knowledge match the requirements of the job.

TYPES OF LEARNING

Learning is generally defined as a process that involves interaction between an organism and the environment and that results in a relatively permanent change in behavior. On a more precise and technical level, learning is defined as a change in the strength of the relationship or connection between a stimulus and a response. A stimulus-response or S-R relationship is a habit, and learning involves either an increase or a decrease in the strength of a habit. We can learn to light up a cigarette in response to stimuli that signal a coffee break or the end of a meal. We can also learn not to smoke in response to these stimuli, and this latter case can be interpreted as a weakening of the smoking habit.

This is the mainstream definition of learning. Not everyone likes it. We saw, for example, that Skinner sees learning less as a *change* in S-R relationships and more as an *increase* in the frequency of a new behavior.

Learning theorists generally distinguish between three types of learning: instrumental learning and classical conditioning fall within the behaviorist tradition and observational learning within the cognitive one. For comparison purposes the major characteristics of the three types are presented in Exhibit 6-1. The reader may notice certain similarities between this new exhibit and Exhibit 2-3, which differentiated the cognitive and behaviorist approaches.

Exhibit 6-1
Types of Learning

Behaviorist school		Cognitive school
Operant	Classical	Observational
Skinner	Pavlov	Bandura
reinforcer: experienced drive reduction (deficit needs) or satisfaction (growth needs)	reinforcer: unconditioned stimulus	vicarious reinforcer: observed drive reduction or satisfaction
reinforcer follows response	reinforcer precedes response	reinforcer, if any, follows response
eliciting stimulus is either undefined or specific	eliciting stimulus is specific	eliciting stimulus is either undefined or specific
reinforcer strengthens or weakens response	reinforcer strengthens response	reinforcer strengthens or weakens response

Instrumental Learning

Instrumental learning is probably the most familiar type of learning. A very simple example, shown in Exhibit 6-2, is that of a new waiter. He may wonder why the work is so hard when the wages are so low. The restaurant owner tells him: You can earn more than your wages in tips. The new waiter, through trial and error, is likely to learn ways of increasing the frequency and size of his tips. He may learn that customers he has served with a smile leave dollar bills rather than coins.

Exhibit 6-2
Examples of the Three Learning Paradigms

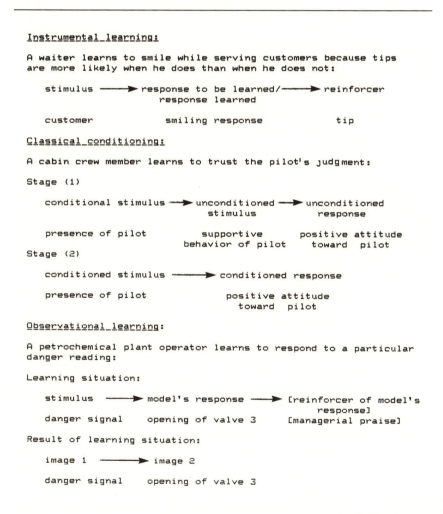

```
Instrumental_learning:

A waiter learns to smile while serving customers because tips
are more likely when he does than when he does not:

    stimulus ──────► response to be learned/──────► reinforcer
                         response learned

    customer              smiling response              tip

Classical_conditioning:

A cabin crew member learns to trust the pilot's judgment:

Stage (1)

    conditional stimulus ──► unconditioned ──► unconditioned
                                stimulus            response

    presence of pilot         supportive        positive attitude
                           behavior of pilot       toward  pilot
Stage (2)

    conditioned stimulus ──────► conditioned response

    presence of pilot                positive attitude
                                         toward  pilot

Observational_learning:

A petrochemical plant operator learns to respond to a particular
danger reading:

Learning situation:

    stimulus  ──────► model's response ──────► [reinforcer of model's
                                                        response]
    danger signal      opening of valve 3      [managerial praise]

Result of learning situation:

    image 1  ──────► image 2

    danger signal      opening of valve 3
```

In practice, instrumental learning processes are usually complex. We say things like "Johnny has learned to find his way to school." However, to the psychologist this type of assertion is an oversimplification. What Johnny really has learned is to turn right at the intersection with the tree, to turn left in front of the corner store, and to turn right at the house with the pointed roof. He has formed at least three new S-R connections or habits.

In Johnny's case, the learned responses are overt. The psychologist defines *response* and *behavior* more broadly, however, to include covert responses such as images, thoughts, and hidden emotional responses. Johnny might learn, for example, to respond with vague unease to the big boy who lives in the house with the pointed roof.

Why does Johnny learn to turn right in response to the intersection with the tree? This innocent question is not easy to answer. It leads to a concept that is as important to learning as those of *stimulus* and *response*: the concept of *reinforcer*. It is on the nature of reinforcers and on whether there always is a reinforcer when learning takes place that psychologists can become very argumentative. About the only point on which they agree is that the reinforcer is a stimulus, object, event, or condition that changes the probability that a given stimulus will be followed by a given response.

The simplest explanation of what happens when Johnny learns to turn right in response to the house with the pointed roof is provided by the mechanistic behaviorists who refuse to consider the contents of Johnny's mind, that is, his expectations, intentions, and hopes. The house with the pointed roof is the stimulus of interest; turning right is the response to be learned. The stimulus is transmitted to the sensory cortex of the brain, and the response originates in the motor cortex. Somehow these two areas of the brain must be linked; some neural pathway must be formed that connects them. The nerves for such pathways are in place, but what is required is a change in certain synapses between nerve cells that allow neural impulses to cross them more easily or make it more difficult for them to dissipate. Reinforcers are the agents that make the formation of new pathways possible.

Simplifying the process considerably (some will no doubt say grossly), we can say that if Johnny is repeatedly reinforced with the teacher's praise immediately after turning right in response to the house with the pointed roof, a neural pathway is set up that in turn, in a manner not yet well understood, connects the relevant area of the sensory cortex with the relevant one of the motor cortex.

In this mechanistic view, the infant who seems to cry so stubbornly in order to attain a "goal" of manipulating the mother into appearing on the double with the milk bottle does in fact not cry because of whatever thoughts go through her mind. She cries because a new pathway has been formed in the brain, linking the sensations of discomfort and the response of crying, because in the past the mother repeatedly rewarded the cries and reduced the unpleasant drive state by rushing to the crib with the bottle.

When Johnny turns right in response to the house with the pointed roof he may be reinforced with praise from the teacher. More precisely, the praise follows the response of entering the classroom. The specific response reinforced is the last one in the sequence and the question arises: What reinforces the responses earlier in the sequence? The reinforcer following these earlier responses is more subtle: the sight of familiar stimuli that tell Johnny he is indeed on the right track, on the way to the secure haven called "school." Johnny may feel relieved by these stimuli. They may reduce a need. Johnny may also entertain all kinds of expectations and goals on his way to school. No one would deny their existence, but the behaviorists would treat them as epiphenomena that do not help explain the learning process.

Johnny's learning to find his way to school is an example of instrumental learning because each of his responses is instrumental in bringing him closer to the safety of the school, to his schoolmates, and to the teacher who may laud his accomplishment as if it were equal to that of Magellan finding his way around the tip of South America. Each response learned or about to be learned is part of the paradigm:

$$S \rightarrow R \rightarrow X,$$

where S is the stimulus, R the response, and X the reinforcer. In other words, a stimulus is followed by a response; the response is followed by a reinforcer. Repetition of this sequence leads to a change in the speed, frequency, and vigor with which the learner responds to the stimulus. In Exhibit 6-2 this paradigm appears in the more concrete form in which it applies to the waiter learning the tricks of his trade.

Often there is no specific external signal. In this case the response is emitted rather than elicited and it is said to be an operant rather than a respondent. This particular type of instrumental learning is Skinner's operant learning or operant conditioning. Even in this case, however, there appears to be a stimulus or stimulus complex. Since it is not obvious and specific, we can represent the paradigm of operant conditioning as:

$$[S] \rightarrow R \rightarrow X$$

In instrumental learning we must distinguish not only between the desirability and undesirability of the reinforcer, but also between situations in which the reinforcer is attained and situations in which it is avoided or escaped from. These distinctions generate the four different variants of instrumental learning shown in Exhibit 6-3.

Exhibit 6-3
Reinforcers and Their Effects in Instrumental Learning

Reinforcer	Effect of Reinforcer	
	Desirable effect (stronger S-R connection)	Undesirable effect (weaker S-R connection)
Desirable Stimulus	positive reward: attainment of reinforcer	extinction: nonattainment of reinforcer
Undesirable Stimulus	negative reward: avoidance of, escape from, reinforcer	punishment: "attainment" of reinforcer

The most straightforward of these variants is the case of a desirable reinforcer which is attained. Here we speak of *positive reward*. The seal is rewarded with a piece of fish when it jumps through the hoop; Johnny may be rewarded with praise when he reaches the school; the worker may receive a bonus when he competently executes his tasks. In all of these examples there is a desirable stimulus that reduces some need of the learner and increases the probability that the learned response or the response to be learned will be made.

In the second case, we have an undesirable or negative reinforcer which is avoided or escaped from by means of the response to be learned. Here an S-R relationship is strengthened because the response to be learned allows the organism to avoid or escape an unpleasant stimulus. The rat learns to jump over a hurdle in its shuttle box to escape from an electrified grid on one side of the box; the worker may learn a productivity-enhancing response to avoid the complaints of the supervisor. In this case, there is a *negative reward*.

In the third case, the reinforcer is a desirable stimulus which is not attained. An S-R relationship is weakened because it is not followed by the reinforcer which at one point did follow it. The secretary who used to be told to take the rest of the day off as a reward for particularly efficient behavior may cease being so efficient when a new boss fails to reward effort in the accustomed manner. This case is referred to as *extinction*.

In the fourth and final case we have an undesirable stimulus which is "attained," albeit unwillingly, and which weakens an S-R relationship. This fourth case of instrumental learning involves *punishment*. A noxious stimulus, object, event, or condition, such as an electric shock, can decrease the probability of a response made. A smoker who receives loud complaints every time he lights up in response to the relaxing situation of waiting for a meal in a restaurant may cease to do so. A more dramatic example is that of the dog whose barking decreases because its master swats it with the newspaper whenever it barks. Such undesirable stimuli like complaints and a newspaper on the rump constitute punishments. In the world of work, reinforcers such as reprimands and threats of dismissal are used to decrease undesirable responses such as calling in sick when there is a sale at the shopping center.

Thus there are four types of instrumental learning referred to as positive reward, negative reward, extinction, and punishment. They are not as clearly separate as one might think at first. For example, it is not always obvious whether a negative reward really differs from a positive reward, or whether punishment really differs from extinction. Is the seal jumping through the hoop to avoid hunger or to attain the piece of fish? Perhaps we can argue for the latter on the grounds that the fish is the salient and dominant stimulus.

Another problem is raised specifically by punishment since it elicits new responses which interfere with the response to be weakened. This complicates the picture and makes undesirable stimuli rather unfruitful reinforcers. Among the responses they frequently elicit and that interfere with the learning process are fear, anger, and frustration. Most supervisors are familiar with these responses and would like to avoid them. Learning theory suggests we avoid punishment as long as possible.

Classical Conditioning

The waiter picks up most of his skills through instrumental learning. A very different kind of learning is involved when a cabin crew member learns to trust the judgment of the pilots of the airplanes he flies on. This is the second example shown in Exhibit 6-2.

It is very important to airlines that cabin crews function in an organized manner and trust their pilots. In an emergency there is no time to form committees and make democratic decisions. If a pilot is supportive, knowledgeable, and confidence-inspiring, his demeanor will produce the desired positive attitude. At this stage, it is the behavior of the pilot that produces the desired response. At a second stage, however, the mere presence of the pilot can produce a positive attitude. The positive response has become associated with the pilot rather than with his behavior. A particular cabin member is said to have learned a new response or to have associated a new response to an originally neutral stimulus.

To say that the pilot is a neutral stimulus means that he is a conditional stimulus, that is, a stimulus that under certain conditions can acquire the ability to elicit certain emotional responses. The pilot's supportive behavior is an unconditioned stimulus, that is, a stimulus that elicits a priori an emotional response. Admittedly that is a liberal definition of an unconditioned stimulus. Some learning theorists reserve the term for stimuli that *reflexively,* not only a priori, elicit an emotional response. Unconditioned stimuli in this more specific sense include electric shock and startling noises.

This second type of learning is called classical conditioning. It is associated with the names Ivan Pavlov and John Watson and its principal feature is an unconditioned stimulus which elicits the response to be learned (to be associated with a new stimulus). This unconditioned stimulus is the reinforcer. It is very different from the reinforcer in instrumental learning not only because it need not be desirable or undesirable, but also because it precedes the response learned or to be learned. The paradigm is:

$$S \rightarrow X \rightarrow R.$$

Here again the behaviorist's interpretation of events is strictly mechanical—the repeated pairing of CS-UCS is assumed to produce a change in synapses linking some sensory center to some center from which the emotional response emanates.

Classical conditioning is particularly important in the development of emotional responses, since these are originally reflexive. Clearly, much learning involves emotional responses. Sometimes the learning is desired, as in the case of the cabin steward. In many cases it is undesired. Supervisors and instructors frequently have to contend with undesired emotional responses acquired earlier. Perhaps the most important reason for considering classical conditioning in the present context, concerned with a broad understanding of work-related processes, is the fact that the ways it differs from the other types of learning throw new light on them.

Observational Learning

Often the training of employees does not involve a reinforcer. The last example of Exhibit 6-2 represents the learning process that takes place when a petrochemical plant operator is simply shown what to do by an experienced worker or supervisor. The learner observes the teacher or model, or more generally observes certain patterns and relationships. That is all. The result of such observational learning is some new or changed association between images, perceptions, expectations, and so forth.

This type of learning is very different from the other two. Instrumental learning and classical conditioning fall comfortably into the parsimonious behaviorist tradition that says "make no assumptions unless you have to, and even then don't if at all possible." Observational learning falls into the cognitive tradition that does not shy away from making assumptions involving human consciousness. It implies that learning need not involve overt instrumental responses or semi-overt emotional ones. The learned response can be a covert one; such learning involves the formation of a connection between the image of a stimulus or situation and the image or idea of the desired response to it.

In science, however, the onus is on those who make new assumptions to show that they are necessary or useful. An interesting study that provided evidence for observational learning is that of Albert Bandura (1965). Each of three groups of children was shown a filmed interaction between an adult and a Bobo doll. The adult slapped and punched the doll. One group saw the adult receive a reward for the aggressive behavior, another saw the adult being punished, and a third saw an adult that received no reinforcement. Note that the children did not receive any reinforcement during this acquisition or learning phase of the study. There was, however, reinforcement for two of the models. From the point of view of the learner, such reinforcement is vicarious reinforcement.

During the test phase of the study, the members of each group were given a Bobo doll to play with. When the children were told they would receive a reward for aggressive behavior, all groups exhibited such behavior. In other words, all three groups had learned the repertoire of aggressive acts merely by watching a model, even though they had not been reinforced. What is more, two of the groups learned in the absence of vicarious positive reinforcement, that is, even when they did not observe a model being rewarded.

This kind of learning suggests that at some point the mechanistic explanation of the behaviorists breaks down. In observational learning, cognitive factors seem to play a role. There is no obvious positive or negative reinforcer, and there certainly is no unconditioned stimulus. Once again we are drawn to the conclusion that it is best to adopt the simplest (i.e., the behaviorist) explanation as long as possible, until it becomes absolutely necessary to consider additional possibilities. The data obtained by Bandura and others do appear to require assumptions beyond those of the behaviorists.

TRAINING METHODS

In the context of ability, we can speak of an interaction between an able individual and an enabling environment. The person has certain basic abilities on which further training can build and which make the acquisition of additional skills possible. The environment offers training programs involving particular training methods ranging from lectures to sensitivity training. As in the case of motivation, one can ask the question: What is the role of the person and what is that of the environment in generating ability? Again there are those who give most of the credit to the "able person" and others who give it to the "enabling environment."

The focus here is on training rather than education. We have seen that training, according to Peters, differs from education in that it is not necessarily concerned with broadening the awareness and deepening the understanding of the learner. Hinrichs (1976) defines training as "skill enhancement." It is task-oriented and hence quite specific and structured. It is also designed to meet the needs of the work organization or of society rather than those of the learner. The skills needed are, according to Hinrichs, cognitive, motor, and interpersonal in nature.

Learning Principles Used in Training

While learning deals with the individual learner and the acquisition of specific responses, training is concerned with groups of employees, the organizational and even national workforce, and with the acquisition of complex response patterns and knowledge. While learning goes on everywhere and at all times, training is associated with particular environments such as training departments and schools.

More important than such differences is the fact that training clearly depends on the learning processes discussed in some detail in the preceding section. The study of learning of animals and humans under controlled conditions in the psychological laboratory has yielded a number of principles of learning which are applied, in varying degrees, by different trainers.

Trainers use positive rewards to strengthen desired stimulus-response relationships, and they usually prefer such positive rewards to negative ones meant to weaken undesired stimulus-response relationships. Feedback on performance levels is provided to the learner and often used as a reinforcer. Trainers keep in mind that learners must be motivated. They know that if there is no drive, traditional drive-reducing reinforcers cannot be effective and, even if they were, the organism would make few responses in general and hence few desired responses in particular.

Trainers know that the greater the similarity between the training situation and the situation in which the new skills are to be applied, the greater the transfer of learning will be from one to the other. Hence the decreasing emphasis on lectures and the increasing popularity of simulations and case studies. Trainers also know that distributed learning can be more effective than massed learning. A course taught during one hour on Mondays, Wednesdays, and Fridays may be more costly to a college and its students and considerably less convenient to all concerned than one taught during three hours on Wednesday night, but the students are likely to learn more, or more thoroughly, during the distributed three one-hour periods.

Available Training Methods

One way of classifying available training methods or techniques is that of Hinrichs (1976) who distinguished between content methods, process methods, and mixed methods.

Content methods primarily transmit knowledge or information. Cognitive skills are the skills mainly concerned here, although the knowledge of how to do something often improves motor skills as well. The lecture method is probably the best known of the content methods. It is cheap because it can serve the needs of a large audience. On the other hand, it is not tailored to the individual and learners are not forced to acquire material; they are passive receptacles of the instructor's insight and wisdom. It is characteristic of educational institutions, and it seems most suited when the trainees are intrinsically motivated and in training for demanding rather than routine jobs.

Audiovisual methods can be used as aids to the lecture method and as procedures on their own: Films, videotapes, overhead projection, and charts make it easier to transmit information to large groups of people, especially when the same material is transmitted to many groups. Add more technology and you enter the area of programmed instruction (PI) and of computer-assisted instruction (CAI). PI is based on Skinner's notion that a correct response will become more likely when it is positively reinforced and that immediate feedback on correct responses is a very effective reinforcer. People like to be told they did it right. CAI enhances the speed with which PI can be developed, displayed, and made to convey complex skills.

Process methods appear to be primarily methods used in developing the interpersonal skills required of managers and supervisors. Cognitive skills are also involved; specific insights or awarenesses may develop. It is difficult to draw the line between cognitive and interpersonal skills. Greater awareness of one's own likes and dislikes, of one's reactions to others, may be the key to more skillful handling of interpersonal relationships. These social awarenesses and interpersonal skills are especially important to managers and supervisors. The former are often said to be leaders rather than "experts"; their technical knowledge is frequently deemed less important than their ability to organize and handle others in effective teams. The talents of the "gamesman" (Maccoby, 1976) are deemed more important than those of the craftsman; senior managers often let others worry about how the work gets actually done.

This means that they must have the skills to recognize their own biases and irrational tendencies, to foresee conflict, to recognize possibilities of effective cooperation. Hinrichs mentions role playing, sensitivity training, and modeling as the main process training methods. Role playing may involve putting oneself in the role of a supervisor face to face with an irate customer; sensitivity training is likely to have no agenda and to concentrate on the famous "here and now" of pleasant or, more typically tense interaction with other group members. It is usually involving, and it can be stressful and produce psychological reactions. It certainly requires highly qualified personnel to sort out the disturbances that may develop. Modeling could involve filmed or live demonstration of skills; it primarily involves Bandura's special observational kind of learning.

Finally, there are the mixed techniques. They combine both the transmission of information of content methods and the changes in attitude and increased awareness of the process methods. In addition, they can promote motor skills (the skills required in manipulating things in the environment critical in traditional work that is now increasingly being done with devastating accuracy by robots).

Conference discussion methods allow for feedback. They are flexible but also expensive. In practice they are reserved for employees at the managerial level in which a work organization is willing to invest sizable resources. Simulation techniques and case studies are widely used in law schools and business schools; they complement the more passive learning initiated by lectures. One advantage of these methods is that they are similar to real life as it will have to be faced by the trainees, although business graduates complain that they do not make strategic decisions once they graduate. Not everyone can be a CEO, after all. But generally there is considerable transfer, for example, in the case of training operators of complex equipment ranging from trucks, Boeing 747s, and nuclear plants to space capsules.

Computers dramatically enhance simulations and case studies. Particularly the former are sometimes hard to differentiate from games, a fact that explains the involvement, emotion, and enthusiasm they can generate. One interesting form of simulation is in-basket training in which the management trainee is given an in-basket with memoranda and letters raising knotty problems and imposing deadlines.

The many varieties of on-the-job training (such as apprenticeships, coaching, or mentoring) and the use of performance appraisals as an adjunct to training (relying primarily on the principle that feedback on performance is beneficial) also fall into this category of mixed training methods. Job rotation deserves specific mention here since it is very popular in Japan, where lifetime employment in the multinationals makes it imperative that employees be able to fill several niches so their employer can respond to changing circumstances with unchanging personnel.

There certainly is a wide palette of training methods available. Whether they are used effectively by the many training environments discussed in the previous chapter is an open question. It seems certain, however, that tougher overseas competition has led to some reevaluation of the importance of optimally trained people at all levels of the American work organization.

7.

Approaches to Competence

The brusque question "What is competence?" is likely to generate confusion and disagreement. It is difficult to define competence, yet every car owner can distinguish between a competent mechanic who deftly manipulates the car until it runs again and an incompetent one who tinkers with it for hours and then presents a big bill and a car that still offers the jerky ride of a willful mule.

Whatever competence is, it manifests itself in work that is easily recognized as exhibiting high quality. The Omega quartz watch that is accurate within seconds over periods of several years was neither designed nor assembled by incompetents. Thus, while we may not be able to define competence in a snappy sentence or two, we can point to examples of the quality in which it results. In other words, it is difficult to define competence and quality conceptually, but we can define them ostensively, by pointing to examples of them.

But what about the competence that leads to such quality? Some people do not think that it is meaningful to regard competence as a human characteristic. To them the quality of work that people do is never a clearly recognizable function of the individual worker. It is always the result of a complex interaction among workers, tools, the education system, the nature of the work task, and the work atmosphere.

Others regard competence as hopelessly subjective. Like art, it strikes them as something that does not exist out there, as something that exists only in the eye of the beholder.

Still others are not convinced that competence is a good thing. The counterculture of the 1960s despised it as an expression of what was perceived as deadening technology interfering with creativity and limiting the freedom to "do one's thing." Competence, unlike "growth" and "self-actualization," was definitely not a glamour word. The counterculture produced phrases like "mere competence," for example, the "mere competence" of an accountant who does not live, but juggles numbers to make a living. The most extreme manifestations of the general disdain for competence were the communes of what in the 1960s and the early 1970s was referred to as "the movement." As Robert Houriet observed, there were in these communes "everywhere cars that wouldn't run and pumps that wouldn't pump because everybody knew all about the occult history of tarot and nobody knew anything about mechanics" (cited from Greeley, 1972, 42). One might note parenthetically that even the most avid fans of the counterculture did not object to a competent pilot while they were airborne, or to a competent surgeon while they lay on the operating table.

The constructs *motive* and *ability* have been examined individually in the preceding chapters. In this chapter, the focus is on the combination or "product" of the two. The order of the chapters on motivation and ability is meant to suggest that the former is somehow more basic than the latter. "There can be no mental development without interest," declares Whitehead. "Interest is the *sine qua non* for attention and comprehension" (1929, 41).

The sparks of interest that characterize what Whitehead calls the "stage of romance"—the first stage of learning, in which the learner exhibits an open mind and enthusiasm—initiate play or more directed and structured development of skills, abilities, and knowledge. As soon as there is ability, however, it in turn affects motivation. Specifically, there is positive feedback from ability to motivation. An increase in ability leads to an increase in self-confidence. This self-confidence is an outcome with an intrinsically positive valence; it thus reinforces further efforts to acquire new abilities and to perfect old ones.

Good teachers, according to Whitehead (1929), set tasks that can be attained to provide "the stimulus of intermediate successes." These further the learner's self-confidence and make it seem worthwhile to tackle more complex tasks. In general, as self-confidence increases, so do the learner's performance-outcome expectancies that performance will produce the intended results and is therefore worth the effort. (See Lawler, 1973.) At this stage, motivation leads not only to play or structured learning, but also to the application of acquired abilities on the job.

While motivation may come first, ability is an equally necessary condition of competence. In fact, in ordinary English the words *competence* and *ability* are often equated. Capable individuals are regarded as competent, regardless of whether the spirit moves them to apply their abilities. Psychologists like Robert White, on the other hand, see competence primarily as a motivational construct, as the expression of a deeply rooted need to deal effectively with one's environment.

But there is clearly much more to be said about competence than that it is the product of motivation and ability. What is needed are insights about competence that add substance to what up to this point is a rather abstract variable. Psychology has a number of such insights to offer.

CRAFTSMANSHIP

When looking for examples to which we can point to illustrate and ostensively define the elusive entity called competence, we often think of craftsmen. One of the finer examples of craftsmanship was portrayed on the British Broadcasting Corporation's TV series, shown on the Public Broadcasting System's network, called *The Duchess of Duke Street*. Louisa, the heroine, is a cook who learns early in her career, and who never forgets, that you use simple materials but the best, and that to get the best you have to go to the market yourself to buy everything "down to the last potato."

Two of the most important characteristics of craftsmanship is the willingness to do small things well and to do things one at a time. This makes the craftsman something of an anachronism in our age of haste and vague holistic visions. The quality of the work we do is largely a function of time, and there seems to be an inability or unwillingness on the part of both workers and the army of students crowding the schools and colleges preparing to join the workforce to allot generous amounts of time to their work.

Two different kinds of time are involved here: the time taken to complete a job and the time taken to acquire the ability to do our jobs well. The first reflects the motivation with which work is approached and executed. Whether we are thinking of the craftsmanship of a potter, of a careful engineer, of a quality-oriented executive, or of a doctor who renders quality service, it connotes an unhurried pace that is in sharp contrast with that of trendy multitaskers flitting from project to project like a bird from flower to flower.

The second kind of time that determines the level of the quality of our work is the time invested in acquiring and developing the abilities it requires. The craftsman who makes his living through his craft has a certain willingness to "stick to his last" and to patiently develop his skills. This willingness makes him a professional rather than an amateur, a football player rather than a flower sniffer. He shares this willingness with doctors who have endured the grind of medical school, professional baseball players who spend years perfecting skills barely visible to the untrained eye, and Olympic athletes who drop everything to pursue a faint glimmer of gold in the distance.

Professionals have their weaknesses, like the tunnel vision that allows them to ignore the danger of nuclear plants which could "go critical" and "melt down." But they are good at what they do. It is in this respect that the craftsman is a professional. In this complex and rapidly changing world, he is a master of something and distinguishes himself from the majority by not fumbling around.

Professionals, competent workers, and craftsmen have practiced their skills to the point at which they have become automatic and require little further attention. Beyond this point it is style that matters. An "old pro" is admired for his "flair," while the amateur is thought of as lacking style and class. "Whoever," Whitehead asks disparagingly, "heard of the style of an amateur painter, of the style of an amateur poet?" (1929, 24).

Psychologists think of styles as deeply ingrained and unconscious ways of doing things. Styles cannot be faked and relate to how things are done rather than to what is done. They manifest themselves in how we write, how we talk, how we dress. They are important enough to cause one poet to exclaim: "Le stile est l'homme même" (The style is the man). In Whitehead's words, style "pervades the whole being. . . . the artisan with a sense for style prefers good work" (1929, 23-24). Style, that most faked and least able to be faked human characteristic, may be the ultimate manifestation of ability, and the time allotted to tasks may be the ultimate manifestation of motivation.

EFFECTANCE

Sometime during the last years of the nineteenth century, the German scientist Karl Groos observed what he called "the child's joy in being a cause" (cited from White, 1959, 316). His observation was an early hint in the emerging new science of psychology that human beings are not just reactive, do not just respond to internal and external emergencies or states of tension. Human beings may sometimes be active rather than reactive. Their behavior is sometimes best described from the subjective point of view and as determined by "personal determinants." They have not only viscerogenic needs but also neurogenic ones.

Both animals and humans sometimes seem to generate activity just for the fun of it. Humans, in particular, often appear to do things that increase rather than reduce drive. For example, they sometimes seek thrills in amusement parks and, alas, on the road. Much of the infant's activity, exploration, and manipulation is accompanied by signs of contentment and cheerful mischief, rather than tension. The infant vigorously thrashes about, emits a wide range of noises, grunts, and yells, and incessantly shakes its rattle.

White dedicated years of thought and research to "the child's joy in being a cause." He noted that the

theory that we learn what helps us to reduce our viscerogenic drives will not stand up if we stop to consider the whole range of what a child must learn . . . . It is not hard to see the biological advantage of an arrangement whereby these many learnings can get under way before they are needed as instruments for drive reduction. [1960, 102]

That things other than drive reducers can produce satisfaction is quite evident to the observer of child behavior. White notes that the fumbling child, smearing his porridge all over his face and chair,

gets more food by letting mother . . . [feed him], but by doing it himself he gets more of another kind of satisfaction—a feeling of efficacy, and perhaps already a growth of the sense of competence. [p. 110]

White's position that there are nonorthodox, nontraditional, neurogenic needs has become increasingly popular in the course of the last 20 years. One reason may be that the Age of Aquarius was less willing to endure the straightjacket of simple one-principle theories to which many of our experiences have to be fitted in a Procrustean fashion. Another may have been an increasing reaction to the focus of psychology on imbalance, maladjustment, and psychopathology, and its neglect of the healthy, active, and effective person that cheerfully explores and manipulates.

According to White (1959), the happily active child seems to experience what Henry Murray and Clyde Kluckhohn (1953) refer to as "pleasure in activity for its own sake" and to exhibit what Karl Bühler (1924) called *Funktionslust*—a simple desire to function. White maintains that "the brain is not simply a mechanism but a living organ that is inherently inclined toward activity" from which "springs the restless urge to find out about the environment and to test the effects of actions upon it" (1976, 215).

Thus White argues that activity, exploration, and manipulation cannot be explained by saying that they reduce physiological drive. They are drives in their own right, albeit nonorthodox ones to increase rather than decrease stimulation, neurogenic rather than viscerogenic in nature. Activity is the basic one among these new drives. It gives rise to exploration on one hand and manipulation on the other. These nonorthodox drives may explain why infants exhibit enough energy to exhaust their parents; why the child comes home with a new bruise every day; why Faust sold his soul to the devil for knowledge, power, and thrills; and why the Portuguese and Spanish ships headed toward Africa, Asia, and America in the fifteenth century.

The new drives to be active, to explore, and to manipulate have much in common. White (1959) refers to them collectively as "effectance motivation," and he defines effectance motivation as a general urge to "interact effectively with . . . [the] environment" (p. 297). He point out that it

is in no sense a deficit motive. We must assume it to be neurogenic, its "energies" being simply those of the living cells that make up the nervous system. . . . We might say that the effectance urge represents what the neuromuscular system wants to do when it is otherwise unoccupied or is gently stimulated by the environment. [P. 321]

As the child grows up, effectance motivation differentiates into specific motives that are clearly related to competence. Different psychologists have labeled these specific motives differently. White speaks of "motives such as cognizance, construction, mastery, and achievement" (1959, 323), and he points out that William McDougall (1923) had identified an "instinct of curiosity"; Ives Hendrick (1942) had written about the "instinct to master"; and Eric Erikson (1953) had introduced the notion of a "sense of industry" that develops in children during the early school years.

All of this means that there is a close relationship between activity, exploration, and manipulation on one hand and the acquisition of the ability, skill, and knowledge that play an important part in determining competence on the other. The former thus have survival value and constitute, to use White's term, a "biological advantage." This biological significance of effectance motivation may be the most convincing reason for arguing that it not only exists, but plays an important role. Its biological raison d'être appears to be as important as that of our tendency to learn and do whatever reduces hunger, thirst, or sexual drive.

Although White refers mainly to evidence from animals, infants, and young children, it seems clear that there is a close relationship between his effectance motivation and Max Weber's (1958) Protestant ethic. One link between White and Weber emerges in the form of Benjamin Franklin, who has attracted the admiring attention of both. White (1976) is fascinated by Franklin's high level of competence and high personal sense of competence. Franklin was extremely effective in dealing with both the physical and social environments. Among other things he invented the Franklin stove and the lightning rod, and he skillfully formulated and applied social skills in a manner that made him the Dale Carnegie of his day.

With that Protestant vigor and industriousness dear to Weber, Franklin put his entire formidable array of competencies in the service of productive work that benefited both himself and those around him. It is no accident that Franklin is a symbol of both White's effectance and Weber's classical, disciplined, and restrained Protestant spirit.

INTERNAL CONTROL

Groos' "joy in being a cause" is related to another area of interest to psychologists: to the domain of attribution theory. This is an area of investigation that seeks to explain how we attribute characteristics and intentions of people, and the causes of events and outcomes, to ourselves, to others, and to the physical environment.

We may, for example, perceive one of our co-workers as the cause of his actions and another as the victim of circumstance. In other words, we may attribute causality to the first but not to the second. Specific other persons may thus be perceived as targets of two kinds of controlling forces—those that emanate from within the person and those that are external in origin. People in general may also be perceived as targets of either internal or external forces. Here we get into philosophical views on the human condition.

But a third perceived target of internal and external forces is of greater relevance here: one's own self. Some people perceive themselves generally as the causes of their own actions; others see themselves as the victims or pawns of forces beyond their control.

Psychologist Julian Rotter distinguished between these two groups and called the first "internals" or "internally controlled" and the second "externals" or "externally controlled." The internally controlled person "perceives that [events are] contingent upon his own behavior or his own relatively permanent characteristics," while the externally controlled one perceives reinforcements as things that follow "some action of his own" but that are not "entirely contingent" on it, that depend to some degree on "luck, chance, fate, . . . and powerful others" (1966, 1).

Internals and externals score at opposite ends of Rotter's (1966) Internal-External Locus of Control scale. This scale consists basically of 23 pairs of statements. One member of each pair reflects a belief in internal control and the other reflects a belief in external control. The more of the external statements a respondent chooses as describing his or her beliefs, the higher the score will be.

Externals resemble learners in a situation arranged to make it appear that the obtained rewards are not contingent on the learner's behavior, that is, that learning is taking place under chance conditions. Internals, on the other hand, are like learners operating under "skill conditions," a situation arranged to make it appear that the reward depends on whether or not the learner makes the correct response.

There are two things to be noted about these learning situations. The reward does not actually have to depend on the correct response. What is important is that the subject *thinks* that it does. Often that impression is created by the instructions the psychologist gives at the beginning of an experimental learning task. In the long run it is, of course, doubtful whether subjects will believe that the reward is contingent on their behavior, when in fact it is not. Also, the word *reward* has a somewhat different meaning in psychology than it does in everyday English. Obtaining something desirable, like a glass of ice cold beer on a hot day, is in principle no more a reward to the psychologist than avoiding something undesirable, like a reprimand from the boss. We have encountered this distinction earlier in the context of learning. It will turn out to be important.

The observation that some individuals act as if life unfolded under skill conditions while others act as if it unfolded under chance conditions was the starting point for the internal versus external control dichotomy. Skinner had established that animals will acquire new responses quickly when they are reinforced every time they make the correct response. Under such "continuous reinforcement" they will also quickly cease to make the correct response when it is no longer reinforced. If the animal is reinforced for only some of the correct responses and if the reinforcement is unpredictable, the response of interest is learned more slowly but it then persists longer after reinforcement is stopped.

As a radical behaviorist, Skinner did not take into account cognitions like beliefs and it did not occur to him that human beings with certain beliefs or expectancies might behave differently. In fact, however, they do. When subjects are tested under skill conditions and believe that rewards depend on their own actions, the learned response persists longer after continuous reinforcement than after partial and random reinforcement. Under skill conditions, internals develop the expectation that rewards will be forthcoming if they do the right thing, and this expectation develops more rapidly and persists longer when reinforcement has been continuous. It is as if the internal were saying, "What, no reward? I *always* get a reward when I do things right. No reward must mean that I didn't do it right. I must try harder next time."

If the subjects of an experiment are told that rewards will be administered by a machine programmed to drop a token at randomly selected time intervals, we have a chance condition. In this situation the internal will not develop the expectation that good outcomes will result from doing things right. Externals, on the other hand, generally believe that their rewards are the results of chance or of the system (the politicians, teachers, bosses) beyond their control, regardless of whether the real situation is a skill condition or a chance condition.

This does not explain why there are individual differences, that is, why some people are internals while others are externals, why some act differently under skill conditions and chance conditions while others act as if chance conditions prevailed all the time.

Suppose we have two individuals, Jane and Harry. Jane was raised in a middle-class home by parents who were encouraging inquisitiveness, activity, and exploration. When she did something right and effectively, praise and material rewards were provided. Teachers tend to be middle-class and to respect children (and parents) from the middle class. They too provided positive reinforcement for Jane's effective behaviors. Jane thus developed the self-confident expectation that if she tries hard, she will obtain handsome rewards.

Harry comes from an underprivileged single-parent home. There was no money to provide material rewards and his parent was too busy trying to make ends meet to be able to provide nonmaterial ones. As a result, Harry did not do well in school, a fact that did not surprise his middle-class teachers who expected poor performance from a lower-class child. Rewards were rare and they were not contingent on Harry's deciding to make an effort, especially since Harry increasingly rarely decided to make one.

Jane and Harry differ in two respects: in what Vroom called the effort-performance expectancies and the performance-outcome expectancies.

Jane expects that if she tries, she is likely to succeed. This expectation is a learned stimulus-response relationship. The stimulus is a perceived need to make an effort; the response is the effort itself. The latter is reinforced by intrinsically rewarding successful performance. In the development of this expectation much depends on whether an interested environment structured tasks so that relatively small successes could be attained and skills developed that make more important challenges surmountable later, and whether it provided feedback letting the child know whether performance was successful or not.

Jane also expects that if she is successful, rewards will follow. She expects that if she sells 40 pairs of shoes she will get a job-security-enhancing pat on the back from the appreciative owner or the bonus for best salesperson of the week.

Jane and Harry differ in their expectancies for three reasons:

1. The degree to which rewards were contingent on making an effort and attaining successful performance was much greater in Jane's case. Jane's parents and teachers were there when she did things right and supplied verbal signals of approval or more tangible rewards.

2. The frequency with which rewards were received was far greater in Jane's affluent home than it was in Harry's impoverished one. Harry received few rewards; thus even if all of them had been contingent on effort and success, there would not have been as many opportunities as in Jane's case to learn that effort and success yield rewards.

3. As soon as Jane learned that effort leads to rewards she made an effort more often. Each time she made an effort, there was another opportunity to learn that effort leads to success. In Harry's case, there never was a reason to make an effort, and hence really no opportunity to learn that it can lead to rewards.

None of this means that Jane is an admirable person while Harry is not. This is a misconception that became popular in the early 1980s. The United States experienced a marked shift from the externally controlled view of American society of the Democrats to the internally controlled Republican view. The Democrats, representing constituents who rely on governmental programs and whose reinforcement histories did not lead them to ranches and bungalows in the sunny South, were replaced at the helm by wealthy and confident Republicans who made it and who therefore think others can make it too if they just try. The Harrys were eclipsed by the Janes; the welfare state made way for the entrepreneurs.

One of the best-known among many apologists of the new internally controlled entrepreneurs is George Gilder (1981, 1984). He is not simply an apologist of the rich. He comments quite disdainfully on inherited wealth and distinguishes between being rich and being wealthy. Being rich means to have money, while the ultimate wealth, in Gilder's view, is the spirit to produce useful goods and services (i.e., the faith that one's efforts will lead to worthwhile rewards).

Gilder complains that this keen insight of the ultimately wealthy (who are invariably also rich) is not shared by the unsuccessful, unlucky, or deprived. The latter want governmental regulations to protect them and governmental handouts to help them. These regulations and huge bureaucracies enforcing them and the taxes taking away a portion of one's well-earned reward are only two enemies of internally controlled conservatives like Gilder. There is also the insidious philosophy of egalitarianism that propagates various "myths of discrimination" and refuses to recognize the fact that there are and always will be higher and lower social classes. "In order to move up," writes Gilder, "the poor must not only work, they must work harder than the classes above them" (1981, 68). Or: the function of the rich is to foster "opportunities for the classes below them in the continuing drama of the creation of wealth and progress" (1981, 63).

We have to remember that in large part, on the scientific level, the differences between Jane and Harry are the result of accident, not of intrinsic merit or ability. Raised in the same environment as Harry, Jane would probably be externally controlled as well. Thus the successful entrepreneurs telling the poor to work harder should remember why they are not poor. Is it because someone else created an environment that allowed them to develop the right expectations? Don't the poor deserve the same thing, even if it is the government that has to play a major role in creating that kind of environment? Is the strong faith in personal determinants exhibited by many conservative and wealthy persons pleased with themselves and their lot simply the opposite and equally unhelpful extreme of the "immediate environment monism" in vogue among social scientists a decade or two ago?

ACHIEVEMENT MOTIVATION

One would expect the successful businessman to confidently strive for further achievements and the victimized inner-city dweller and the marginal farmer to throw in the towel. So it is not surprising that Rotter ascribed to "internals" the tendencies to place great value on rewards that have been earned through skill or achievement, to demand recognition for their successes, and to exhibit concern about their failures. These characteristics resemble those attributed to high scorers on measures of the need to achieve developed by David McClelland and his colleagues at Harvard (McClelland et al., 1953). Like White, McClelland was a student of Henry Murray.

But the relationship between internal control and achievement is less clear than this parallel suggests. Correlation coefficients reflecting the degree of relationship between Rotter's Locus of Control scale and McClelland's projective test measure of the need to achieve are low and indicate a weak or complex relationship.

Projective tests involve the presentation of ambiguous stimuli on large cards that are held before the subject. McClelland and his colleagues used cards from the Thematic Apperception Test developed by Murray and his group. This test involves showing the subject a number of scenes depicted in fairly ambiguous ways. On one famous card, for example, a boy sits at a table and pensively looks at a violin lying in front of him. The subject is instructed to tell a story about what led up to the scene on the card. In the story of a subject high on the need to achieve, the boy might appear as a young music student nervously awaiting the marks awarded by the jury of a competition in which he has just finished his performance, and resolving to practice harder no matter what the outcome of the competition in order to become the best violinist in the country. A low achiever, on the other hand, might tell a story about a boy who would prefer to play with his friends than practice for his next parentally imposed violin lesson.

Whether there is a direct relationship or not, there seems to be little doubt that both internal control and the need to achieve are related to competence. Competence requires the motivation to acquire abilities and to master skills, and the need to achieve and the belief that one's effort will very likely lead to the intended and desirable results appear to be prime sources of that required motivation. (See Clark, 1969, 4.)

PERSONAL CAUSATION

The work of Richard deCharms (1968) is related to these empirically well-established constructs of internal versus external control and the need to achieve. But deCharms goes beyond these concepts by linking them to a broader problem: the question of how action is initiated. This question led him along a path that is different from those of Rotter and McClelland.

Unlike Rotter, deCharms does not stop on the level of cognition, perception, or belief. It is one thing to establish, as Rotter did, that some people think of themselves as causal agents, as capable of having intended effects of the environment. It is another to speculate about the actual processes underlying a person's effects on the environment. As deCharms points out, we are touching on the modern version of the mind-body problem here. The question of interest is no longer simply "What do people believe about their effectiveness in producing desirable outcomes?" Instead, it is "Can human beings initiate chains of events?" This leads to the further questions "If so, how do they initiate change?" and "What is the relationship between people's beliefs about their efficacy as change agents and their real effects on their environment?"

Unlike McClelland, White, and others, deCharms is not primarily concerned with the distinction between mechanistic and organismic views about motivation. He sees both of these models (he calls them the "stimulus reduction" and "arousal" models) as "affect explanations" that differ from something new he proposes to adopt: the "thought-action paradigm." This paradigm is rooted in the use of the Thematic Apperception Test by Murray and McClelland to tap people's less-than-fully-conscious thoughts and fantasies. DeCharms refers to testing by means of the Thematic Apperception Test as "thought sampling" and he implies that thought precedes action and that thought sampling can, therefore, tell us what people are likely to do later based on the thoughts they have now.

The problem of the relationship between thought and action arises particularly clearly in the domain of the motive to achieve because it is, as deCharms notes, "uniquely human." Research on achievement motivation supports the view that human beings not only react, but that they are also proactive; that they not only seek to reduce physiological needs or stimulation, but that they can initiate action that is more a function of themselves than of their environment.

In deCharms' terms, people are capable of personal causation, that is, of "initiat[ing] behavior intended to produce a change in the environment" (1968, 6). This notion of personal causation leads to another notion, that of personal knowledge. Personal causation implies knowledge that such causation is possible. In the absence of such knowledge, it would be pointless to try and produce intended effects on the environment. To go a step further: Such knowledge about the possibility of personal causation must be personal in nature, that is, private knowledge about our own feelings and thoughts. DeCharms points out that only the individual person knows what he or she means by the phrase "I want." And when someone else informs us that "he wants" something, the only reason we know what he means is our knowledge of what we mean when we say "I want." This example is useful in understanding what is meant by attributing causality to oneself and hence the nature of the personal determinants discussed in Chapter 1.

DeCharms also focuses on individual differences. But where Rotter's "internals" and "externals" are low and high scorers on the Locus of Control scale, deCharms discusses two types that are distinct entities differing in many respects. He calls his qualitatively different types "origins" and "pawns." These labels suggest much more than simply a difference in locus of control. They conjure up a vision of a competent "origin" ready to engage in the hard work of developing and using the skills of a craftsman, oozing with effectance motivation, internally controlled, and propelled by a healthy but not exaggerated need to achieve.

PART III.

PERFORMANCE

8.

The Work Environment

We have seen that the term *competence* was not held in great esteem during the years of the counterculture. Given the impetuous and impulsive nature of that culture, that is not surprising. What is somewhat surprising is that the term did not excite much interest within the techno-economic structure either. Even today the literature on management and industrial-organizational psychology rarely mentions it.

The generally romantic, impulsive, and self-oriented culture rejected "mere competence" because it implied gauche precision and unfashionably patient plodding. The techno-economic structure rejected it because managers and entrepreneurs are not really interested in invisible human dispositions and potentials. Competence is something on which they cannot put a value, which they cannot sell. By itself it does not constitute anything of value visible to the naked eye.

Managers are interested in something more tangible than competence: performance. Not only are workers and managers said to perform; so are organizations, machines, programs, and the national economy. Performance results in productivity which, in turn, is the raison d'être of the techno-economic structure.

Just as we need the new element of ability to get from motivation to competence, so we need the new element usually referred to as the "work environment" to get from competence to performance. While there is no need for immediate-environment monism, the environment is as important a determinant of performance as is the person.

The effects of the work environment on work performance are obviously both direct and indirect. The most competent watchmaker cannot function if the illumination is too low: The low illumination may have a variety of effects, but it clearly affects performance directly by making it impossible to discriminate among minuscule parts and features. On the other hand, a drill may require such intensive attention that the worker tires after a few minutes, or the management of a company may be so authoritarian that workers are unable to do their work in what they know to be a better way. Here the effects are more indirect: High stress, and consequent low level of well-being, and a low degree of work satisfaction are likely to result in these cases, and these consequences are important both in their own right and because they can affect performance indirectly.

The work environment was discussed briefly in Chapter 1. Some of its important features, in the views of such industrial and organizational psychologists as Herzberg, Schneider and Locke, and Hacker, were listed in Exhibit 1-1. Exhibit 8-1 focuses on them with greater emphasis and shows some additional details. The conditions and agents with an asterisk are those discussed in more detail in this chapter. This exhibit takes us beyond the worker, who has generally been the subject of the book up to this point.

Exhibit 8-1
The Work Environment

Conditions_intrinsic_in_the_work

* Tasks constituting the job (Hacker's (1978) task-specific working conditions).

  Nature of work process (e.g., is work smooth? sporadic? strenuous?)

  Opportunities for success, promotion, responsibility, verbal recognition

  Means (Hacker's (1978) job-specific conditions)

Conditions_extrinsic_to_the_work

* Physical working conditions (Hacker's (1978) "general spatial-temporal working conditions." Both Hacker and Locke (1973) include work schedules among the physical conditions)

      a. conditions pertaining to space, to the workplace

      b. conditions pertaining to time

  Compensation (money)

  Interpersonal atmosphere

Agents_extrinsic_to_the_worker:_Social_working_conditions

* Management, supervisors, subordinates (Leader-follower relationships)

  Co-workers

  Customers

Note: The aspects of the work environment with an asterisk are those pursued in more detail in the text. The table is not meant to include all relevant aspects of the work environment.

To get the whole picture of performance we must now look at the work environment and then at the output of the system comprising worker and work environment.

CONDITIONS INTRINSIC IN THE WORK

The most immediate environmental determinants of work behavior are the work tasks facing the worker. These may range from the demanding tasks involved in making a medical diagnosis to the routine tasks of attending a conveyor belt in a bottling plant. The task is usually defined by the employer, directly and in detail in the case of the assembly line worker, in the form of objectives and guidelines in the case of the typical professional. Deadlines may have to be met, norms may have to be fulfilled, certain abilities and knowledge may be called for.

Finding out what the work tasks associated with a job are is the function of job analysis. Ernest McCormick and Daniel Ilgen follow the U.S. Employment Service in defining *job* as "a single position or group of similar positions in one establishment, in which the work activities and objectives are similar . . . [while differing] significantly from those of other positions" (1985, 40). It is something between the position of an individual and an occupation encompassing many jobs in different work organizations. All bakers have the same occupation, but one may work in his own small shop, and another may mix dough in a large plant. The job is thus something that is specific enough to permit detailed analysis and permanent enough to be *worthy* of analysis.

The job analyst needs to find out what holders of the job (incumbents) do or should do, what the job elements are. This can be done by questioning the incumbents, their supervisors, or others familiar with the work. This can also be done by observing people doing the job, and sometimes the analyst can do the job him- or herself for a while. The objective of formal job analysis is to obtain a quantitative job description that will allow comparison of jobs with each other and the computation of indices of relationship between their components and a variety of other variables such as work motivation and ability levels. For this reason information is usually obtained by asking about jobs with structured questionnaires which yield quantifiable results.

McCormick (1959) has distinguished between job-oriented work tasks such as "grinds castings" and "galvanizes sheet metal" and worker-oriented activities such as "manually pours ingredients into container" and "observes conditions of product in process." Note that the latter refer to fairly general activities that are shared by many different jobs.

Job analysis questionnaires that are structured and job-oriented list work tasks to be performed by the incumbent. Such checklists are often developed by asking incumbents to list critical incidents on the job. For example, if several incumbents indicate that they almost burned themselves when they dropped the soldering iron, the job analyst may have an item for the checklist: "handles soldering iron."

Probably the most widely used example of a worker-oriented structured job analysis questionnaire is the Position Analysis Questionnaire (PAQ) (McCormick, Mecham, and Jeanneret, 1977). Two of its job elements are "use of written materials" and "coding/decoding information." Worker-oriented questionnaires of this type permit the job analyst not only to describe a specific job, but also to make comparisons, useful in such areas as personnel selection and training, between different jobs.

To recapitulate: Of the various ways of obtaining job information, the most frequently used is to ask those who know the job well. We can ask about a job informally or systematically, and in a job-oriented or more general and generalizable worker-oriented way as is done with the PAQ. The PAQ illustrates job analysis at its most formal and advanced.

The authors of the PAQ began with a general framework of work behavior based on the Stimulus-Organism-Response model focusing on the obtaining of information needed to do the job, the processing of that information, and the resulting output or actual work behavior. This framework provided three categories of job elements. Other categories were added: job elements pertaining to the relationship with others at work, working conditions, and a miscellaneous category of other unclassifiable job elements.

These six categories are not elegant, mainly because there is no single basis for classification. The first three categories are based on a model that is not related to the remaining three. In spite of that, the classification schema served the purpose of generating ideas about what aspects of work behavior to look at to identify job elements. It allowed McCormick and his colleagues to identify 194 job elements.

The PAQ lists these 194 job elements and calls for a rating of each of them based on the job being analyzed. Several different rating scales are used. For example, the rating scale ranging from *no use* to *very frequent use* is the one called for by the item "written material." Suppose the job analyzed is that of mail clerk. The item "written material" would probably be rated *frequently used*, since addresses, postal tariff tables, and instruction manuals have to be read frequently. The job element "coding/decoding information" is rated on a scale ranging from *not important* to the job to *very important* to the job. In the case of the mail clerk who has to read zip codes it might be rated as *important* to the job. The PAQ ratings may be done by the job analyst familiar with the job, by the job holder, or by a supervisor. Often they are done as a collaborative effort, in the course of an interview conducted by the job analyst with the incumbent.

Clearly, 194 job elements do not provide a clear overview of what the job involves. Statistical analysis of these items allows the identification of groups of items. These empirical groups of items need not, and do not, correspond to the categories employed at the outset of the development of the PAQ. The latter have served their heuristic purpose. What is of interest now is not which job elements appear to go together rationally, but which items actually do go together empirically.

In one of several analyses, most of the 194 job elements of the PAQ were correlated and factor analyzed. Factor analysis is a statistical procedure that allows one to account for the relationships between an unmanageably large number of variables by means of a small number of broader underlying dimensions. Application of this procedure yielded 13 groups of items of which the largest and most important ones were the three consisting of items referring to "decision-making, communication, and general responsibilities," "operating equipment and machinery," and "clerical/related activities," respectively. These broad dimensions or job components constitute the meaningful aspects on which different jobs can be compared and which can be used to establish relationships between jobs and variables such as abilities, health indices, and so forth.

Although industrial and organizational psychologists seem to define it somewhat more broadly, for our purposes it is best to think of job analysis as a set of activities that results in a job description. In other words, the term is used here in a restricted sense to refer only to the identification of job elements, not to that of required worker characteristics. The latter implies inferences from the job elements and appears to constitute a distinct additional step.

Most job descriptions contained in recruitment advertisements in newspapers and other media are informally developed by managers. However, formal job analyses and formally obtained job descriptions are important for a variety of reasons. From the point of view of this book they are particularly important in criterion development and in matching people and jobs.

Job analysis data provide the basis on which criteria can be developed. Criterion development is a central activity in industrial and organizational psychology. Criteria are indicators of success. Without good criteria it is impossible to evaluate, and we need to evaluate such things as the performance of individual employees, the outcomes of our attempts to match people and jobs, the productivity of a department or firm, and the effectiveness of different training methods. Note that in every case it is performance that is evaluated.

Job analysis data also provide one of the bases for matching people and jobs. The main objective of this matching process is to optimize performance. Some strategies focus on fitting people to jobs. Here the job description is used in recruitment ads to find people who can do the required job tasks and in identifying training needs to change available personnel so they can fit the job better. Other strategies concentrate on fitting the job to people. Here we need to know what the job is so we can decide which of its elements should be changed.

CONDITIONS EXTRINSIC TO THE WORK

The most important conditions that fall into this category are the physical working conditions. They are frequently the cause of stress and dissatisfaction. They include variables characterizing the space around the worker (the workplace) as well as variables physical in the sense that they have to do with time but that originate in such aspects of the work environment as the supervisor who sets up work schedules. Hacker (1978) refers to both types of physical conditions as the "general spatial-temporal working conditions."

Physical Conditions Pertaining to the Workplace

The physical working conditions are typically the concern of the engineer. The handbooks of the Illuminating Engineering Society and the American Society of Heating, Refrigerating and Air-Conditioning Engineers, for example, provide standards of illumination and temperature. A third major factor is noise. Standards regarding noise have been established by the U.S. Occupational Safety and Health Administration.

Illumination

Illumination may be particularly relevant in the age of the video display terminal (VDT). Complaints about the eyestrain it is said to cause abound. The computerized work station can be stressful: The eyes dart from the keyboard, to the hard copy draft, to the screen, and perhaps to the printer (*In the chips*, 1982). In addition, VDTs easily produce glare. Glare is any annoying and tiring brightness in the field of vision. Direct glare is produced by sources of illumination that are within the field of vision rather than above or behind the worker; indirect glare is produced by surfaces in the field of vision reflecting more than an optimal amount of light. The worker operating a VDT may have to contend with both types of glare. The display itself is a source of light and the shiny glass surface of the cathode ray tube constituting the display may reflect sources of light behind the worker.

There are two units of measurement that are useful in specifying optimal illumination levels. The footcandle is the unit of direct light, of illumination. It is the amount of light received one foot away from a "standard" candle. The footlambert is the unit of reflected light, of luminance. The two are related: A footlambert is the amount of light reflected by a uniform square that is perfectly white and perfectly diffusing, and one foot away from a 1-footcandle light source.

Different work tasks obviously call for different levels of illumination. A major factor in determining the amount required is the task contrast, the figure-ground reflectance difference. Another factor is the size of the objects or symbols manipulated or used in the work. These factors tend to increase the level of illumination required for work in the hospital operating room: A high 500 footcandles may be called for. They tend to push it down for work in the typical hotel lobby. There 10 footcandles may suffice.

Temperature, Humidity, and Pollution

Temperature and humidity are two important atmospheric working conditions because they affect body temperature, a temperature that is generated by the body's metabolism, particularly in the course of physical work. The problem is to create conditions that optimize body temperature. The environment can affect body temperature in several different ways. The most obvious is convection through which air or water transfers heat to or from the body. Another is evaporation: As perspiration evaporates on the skin it consumes heat and cools adjacent tissue.

The humidity of the atmosphere is a major factor affecting body temperature. When it is high, evaporation does not work as a cooling mechanism. The air simply contains too much moisture to absorb more. Because they are closely linked, air temperature and humidity are considered together. One index that reflects their combined effects is the Wet-Bulb Globe Temperature (WBGT). A somewhat complex instrument is used to obtain two readings: dry-bulb temperature and wet-bulb temperature. The dry-bulb temperature is obtained by a normal thermometer; the wet-bulb temperature reading is obtained from a bulb that is surrounded by a wick connected to a small water reservoir. The wick evaporates water, creating an atmosphere with a relative humidity of 100 percent around the wet bulb. If the relative humidity of the atmosphere is 100 percent also—that is, if the air contains all the water moisture it can hold at a given temperature—then the two readings are the same. The WBGT is a weighted average of the two readings.

The heavier the work, as measured by the kilocalories (the "calories" of everyday English) it consumes per hour, and the higher the WBGT, the greater the need for rest periods. For example, if the WBGT is 86 degrees Fahrenheit and the work is heavy work that requires 500 kilocalories per hour, people should work only 25 percent of each hour and rest during the remainder of the time (Dukes-Dobos and Henschel, 1971, cited from McCormick and Ilgen, 1985).

Of course the example of high temperature is merely one of many examples of atmospheric conditions that impinge on the worker and affect work behavior. Low temperature has a range of effects that are quite different from those of high temperature. The effects of low temperatures on manual dexterity have been experienced by many who tried to tie their skates or adjust their ski bindings on a cold winter day. It may also be familiar to many who are the victims of an air conditioning system that generates arctic conditions in the middle of July.

Air pollution is another atmospheric condition that affects worker well-being, work behavior, and presumably performance. It is a more subtle problem than in the old days of coal. However, technology did not only give us cleaner methods of heating and production, it also introduced thousands of new chemicals. These quietly enter the atmosphere in minute quantities whose total effect is not minute at all. They are likely to stay there because in the large modern office towers the intake and exhaust of air is controlled by a central system. The windows cannot be opened, partly because open windows prevent the air conditioning system from doing its job and maybe because there is fear that objects thrown from high towers could lead to injury and lawsuits. As a result of this control of intake and exhaust, the air tends to be recirculated. The central systems are relatively closed systems, since it costs money to cool new, hot air from the outside or to heat new, cool air. Fresh air, or at least new air, is often introduceed as if it were a most precious resource. The result is pollution, lack of oxygen, and other less-than-optimal conditions.

Noise

Noise has been defined as sound that is irrelevant to the task at hand (Landy, 1985, 522). Analogous to the distinction between signal and noise in communication theory, one can distinguish between relevant sounds on the job, like the instructions of a foreman, and noise.

Noise has two kinds of effects: As most rock fans find out, it can impair hearing temporarily or permanently. Noise levels of 90-120 decibels experienced over a number of years on the job by operators of earth-moving equipment, for example, have been shown to produce hearing loss (LaBenz, Cohen, and Pearson, 1967, cited from McCormick and Ilgen, 1985, 410).

The effects of noise on work behavior in general and on work performance in particular are not very clear, however. Noise can distract and arouse. Distraction leads to a decrement in performance. Moderate arousal is likely to improve performance while high arousal is likely to interfere with it. Effects such as distraction and arousal, and ultimately effects on work behavior, depend on the characteristics of the noise, of the work, and of the worker.

Landy distinguishes four characteristics of noise: its amplitude or loudness, its frequency or pitch, its complexity, and whether it is continous or intermittent. The most disturbing noise is probably loud, high-pitched, and intermittent. Routine work may be less affected by noise than is nonroutine work.

The worker is a factor in two distinct ways. First, there are two mechanisms that help workers adjust to noise. They are habituation and auditory adaptation. Both help the worker to adjust to continuous noise; one is relatively central, the other is peripheral (i.e., it takes place in the ear). These mechanisms suggest that *change* in noise level, rather than high noise level, may be most likely to affect performance. Second, there appear to be personality variables that make some workers more vulnerable to noise than others. The trait of introversion versus extraversion may play a role here. It seems far more likely that introverts will complain about noise levels than will extraverts. Introverts typically have an actual arousal level that is above their optimal arousal level, and thus they seek to reduce stimulus input. The opposite is true of the extraverts: They are more likely to complain when noise levels are low because their actual arousal level is usually below their optimal arousal level. They need excitement. The mechanism of *protective* inhibition complicates matters, however. According to Eysenck (1971), this mechanism swings into action in introverts when the noise level moves beyond a certain range of intolerability. At that point they apparently no longer respond to it.

Physical Conditions Pertaining to Time: Work Schedules

The work schedule may be set by the supervisor or by company policy handed down from higher levels. What makes it important is its effects on the physiological state of the worker. Operating under an unsuitable work schedule, the worker may be fatigued, tense, and irritable. This physiological state interacts with the physical working conditions characterizing the workplace. It is a stressor that is likely to interact with other stressors such as excessive noise or interference from co-workers.

Work schedules can differ in a variety of ways. For example, the work hours may be massed or distributed. The work hours of a stewardess on an overseas flight are likely to be massed; those of a bus driver working only during peak periods in the morning and late afternoon would be distributed.

Related to massed versus distributed work hours are issues concerning the four-day versus the five-day work week. Do workers prefer to get their work done in four ten-hour days, or do they prefer the normal five-day week? What kinds of workers would like to get their work out of the way? Not surprisingly, some evidence suggests that younger workers with low-level jobs, low incomes, and low job satisfaction are likely to prefer the four-day concentrated work week.

Then there are issues pertaining to shift work. Which workers prefer steady day-shift? Which ones prefer night-shift? Which workers are able to adjust to rotating shifts, changing their sleep habits easily as they switch from day-, to afternoon-, to night-shift at regular intervals? There is evidence that relatively few people can handle rotating shift work because of the deeply ingrained circadian rhythm that makes most of us alert during the time when we can see and hence operate best, namely, during daylight hours. A few workers do well on permanent night-shift or on rotating shift schedules, but apparently only experience can tell who belongs in these groups.

Finally, the work schedule also encompasses the question of rest periods.

Nothing arouses an employer more intensely than the sight of employees at rest during working hours. The distance between employers and employees has increased, at least in the large corporations, but managers tend to think that since rest periods reduce the number of hours worked, they must also reduce output. Research on rest periods in the famous Hawthorne studies (Roethlisberger and Dickson, 1939) constitutes one of the early classics of research on work behavior. It suggests that rest periods need not reduce output and that they may do wonders for job satisfaction.

AGENTS EXTRINSIC TO THE WORKER

Thomas Carlyle's *French Revolution* (1906) shows how particular figures, like Danton, Marat, and Robespierre, emerge and change the course of history by means of concrete interventions ranging from policy decisions to letting heads roll and blood flow through the streets, to oratorical outbursts that swayed the populace and the National Assembly.

In contrast, Leon Tolstoi's *War and Peace* (1942) depicts General Kutuzov, commander of the Russian army at the time of Napoleon's invasion of Russia, as a man whose decisions are shaped by the pattern of events and by the conditions around him. Kutuzov withdraws and ponders and he attacks only when he has to. He allows the climate and the wide spaces of Russia to weaken Napoleon, intervening as little as possible, and going with the flow no matter how anxiously others urge him to confront the French and be a hero.

Carlyle and Tolstoi present two quite different conceptions of leadership.[1] To Carlyle the leader is a hero who changes the course of events; to Tolstoi the leader is created by the circumstances and is essentially a person who is in the right place at the right time. Carlyle clearly emphasizes the role of the person. Tolstoi emphasizes the environment: A hurricane like the invading French allows a Kutuzov, who bends with the wind and who might be considered a coward in other situations, to play an important part and to become a "leader" and "hero" to posterity.

The differing characterization of leaders by Carlyle and Tolstoi provide a starting point for asking basic questions about the nature of leadership. People exercising some kind of leadership are probably the most important of the agents extrinsic to the worker and they are used here to illustrate that third category of determinants emanating from the work environment.

Our starting point leads to the position that there are three basic schools of thought on leadership: There are those who see leadership as a function of the person, those who see it as a function of the situation calling for leadership and selecting leaders who happen to be in the right place at the right time, and those who see it as a function of both person and environment. This is, of course, a familiar set of categories.

Personal Aspects of Leadership

The old-fashioned person-oriented approach is rooted in earlier historical stages when one individual frequently made a significant difference in the way in which events unfolded. Arnold Toynbee (1954), in his monumental *Study of History,* contrasts the Heroic Ages with later stages in the evolution of societies, more civilized stages relying more on the law than on the whims of powerful individuals. The early Greeks and the Germanic peoples have provided the West with epic poetry detailing the exploits of such heroes as Achilles, Odysseus, Dietrich, and Siegfried.

In the stage of what Toynbee calls the "barbarian war-bands," characteristics of independent individuals such as physical strength, martial skills, and a pragmatic intelligence played probably a more important role than they do in the age of computers and complex systems of interdependent parts. But the myths that have grown out of the deeds of these individuals play an important role even today. The dream of being a latter-day Siegfried motivated many a German to fight to the bitter end in 1945.

No one expects the modern manager to be an Achilles or a Siegfried, but McCormick and Ilgen (1985) point out that the traditional approach is not entirely without merit. They refer to a study by Edwin Ghiselli (1971) which found interesting differences between above-average and below-average managers. The above-average managers obtained higher scores on measures of decisiveness, intelligence, and need for self-actualization. They obtained lower scores on the needs for job security and for financial rewards. But in general this trait approach to leadership has not been very productive and it has made way for the behavioral and contingency approaches.

The behavioral approach focuses on what leaders do rather than on what traits they might possess. In other words, this approach is more circumspect; it confines itself to what can be observed and does not care for bold inferences about what the behavior might be a manifestation of. What is of interest are certain consistencies in behavior, certain clusters of behaviors that seem to go together.

This approach has led to the identification of two different behavior patterns exhibited by leaders. These are referred to as leadership styles, although this raises the question of in just what way styles differ from traits. It seems clear that the word *style* in this context is not used as a characteristic of the leader that is as consistent and stable as a traditional personality trait.

Robert Bales (1949) distinguished between *task-facilitative* and *socio-emotional* leadership behavior patterns in small groups. Rensis Likert at the University of Michigan and a group of psychologists at Ohio State University isolated pairs of leadership styles that are similar to that of Bales. Likert (1955) distinguished between *job-centered* and *employee-centered* leaders and Ralph Stogdill and Alvin Coons (1957) between leaders who initiate structure and leaders who exhibit consideration toward followers. The work of Stogdill and his colleagues at Ohio State resulted in two widely used questionnaires, similar in that they measure *structure initiation* and *consideration*, and different in that one, the Leadership Behavior Description Questionnaire, requires subordinates to describe the behaviors of their supervisor, while the other, the Leadership Opinion Questionnaire, is answered by supervisors describing what they think their own behavior should be like.

These two leadership styles are not mutually exclusive. Robert Blake and Jane Mouton (1964) have constructed the *managerial grid* whose two axes are *concern for production* and *concern for people*. They suggest that the leader who is high on both dimensions is most likely to be effective in a wide range of situations.[2]

Of particular interest here, in the context of Japanese competition, is the work of Misumi (1972) who studied a large number of Japanese managers in a wide variety of enterprises. Using measures ranging from productivity indices to accident rates and working in both laboratory settings (to observe short-term effects) and field settings (to study long-term effects), Misumi found that those of his managers high on both *production* and *maintenance* concerns (PM leaders) were in charge of the most productive and satisfied groups.

Misumi's maintenance corresponds to Blake and Mouton's concern for others. It seemed to be more important than the production aspects: The only measures on which the managers who stressed production more than maintenance (Pm leaders) scored higher than the managers who stressed maintenance more than production (pM leaders) were those of short-term productivity and short-term accident rates.

Environmental Aspects of Leadership

This brings us to the environment. Does the situation select or make the leader? Were the actions of Kutuzov dictated by the environment? Did the environment select him for the job of first retreating in orderly fashion and then pursuing the French?

These are not easily answered questions. However, one thing seems certain. The environment in the form of a person's position has a powerful effect on his or her behavior. French social critic Andre Gorz asks:

[Is] the position of domination *created* by its occupant and is the power which it confers destined to disappear along with the individual? Or, on the other hand, is power inherent in the *pre-existing position* occupied by its holder within a system of social relations and is it, as a result, independent of the individual occupying it? [1982, p. 56]

Amitai Etzioni (1961) has pointed out that a leader's total power consists of personal power and position power. Personal power is a function of the leader: perhaps of personality, interpersonal skills, and charisma. Position power, of interest here, is the power that is assigned to the leader by the position held. It increases as the manager moves from positions low in the organizational hierarchy to positions that are on higher levels. Gorz's point seems to be that the proportion of total power that is position power has increased in recent times.

In an aging social structure, Gorz argues, power is associated with positions that constitute what is called "the establishment." In such a society there is no room for adventurers and entrepreneurs. Such a society is hospitable only to careerists interested in climbing up the conventional ladder to a position conferring some power. Gorz argues that "power is an organigramme" (1982, 58) and he sees the faceless bureaucrat following orders as the typical leader type of this kind of society.

While Gorz is highly critical of power associated with position, there is something positive to be said about it as well. Bureaucracy, as Weber (1968) saw it, is a means to get around even greater evils: nepotism, whim, and tyranny. The rules of a bureaucracy, although they do not fit nonroutine situations, can at least assure more equitable treatment in routine situations. Thus the power of leaders is often power the environment grants them, and the fact that they cannot do as they please need not necessarily cause us to shed tears.

The Interaction Between Person and Environment in the Context of Leadership

As in the case of motivation and ability, one must ultimately look at the interaction of the person and the environment (which in large part means "position") in order to understand leadership.

The classic work looking at both person and environment is that of Fred Fiedler (1971), who examined leadership style in relation to three environmental variables. Fiedler measured leadership style by means of the ratings given to the least preferred co-worker, or LPC. High LPC leaders describe even their least preferred co-worker in relatively positive terms; low LPC leaders see little if anything that is good in their least preferred co-workers.

The three environmental variables of interest to Fiedler were leader-member relationships, task structure, and position power. Leader-member relationships are good when the leader is liked by the members of his or her group. Task structure is high when the correctness of solutions can be verified, when the task requirements are specific, and so forth. Finally, position power is high when the leader has legitimate power, that is, power conferred on him or her by, or with the approval of, the members of the group.

Fiedler found that in situations in which these variables are low, creating a difficult situation for the leader, *and* in situations in which they are high, creating a favorable situation, it is the low LPC leader who is likely to be more effective, while situations that are neither favorable nor unfavorable seem to call for a high LPC leader.

This barely scratches the surface of the considerable amount of research that has been done on leadership. The intent here is merely to illustrate the category of social working conditions. It is clear that leadership is a very important social determinant of work performance. Leaders can structure the demands to be dealt with and they can motivate. If they are ineffective, the most competent worker may not be able to perform.

This is true of all aspects of the work environment discussed in this chapter. They constitute conditions that must be met at some minimal level if competence is to be translated into performance. Of course, the workers do not always face the work environment helplessly. Some aspects may be under their control. The more competent the workers, in fact, the less helpless they are likely to be since competence implies, among other things, some ability to cope with less-than-optimal circumstances. Basically, however, the tasks of the job must not demand abilities the workers do not have; the work schedule must be one to which workers can adapt; the workers must be able to see what they are doing, and the leadership of the work organization must know when to intervene and when not to stand in the workers' way to excellent performance.

NOTES

1. The literature on leadership has noted the contrast between Carlyle and Tolstoi. It is essentially the contrast between the "Great Man" theory on the one hand, and "situation," "times," or "Zeitgeist" theory on the other (e.g., Sargent and Williamson, 1966).

2. Early sources on leadership styles are cited here, although I had to rely on secondary sources.

9.

Defining and Measuring Performance

PERFORMANCE ON THE NATIONAL, ORGANIZATIONAL, AND INDIVIDUAL LEVELS

We saw in Chapter 8 that both the counterculture and the techno-economic structure rejected the notion of competence in the 1960s and early 1970s. Within the techno-economic structure the main reason for rejecting it probably was the simple fact that managers and entrepreneurs are not interested in invisible human dispositions and potentials. What managers are interested in is performance, something more tangible and concrete than competence. Not only workers and managers are said to perform; so are organizations, machines, and programs.

Performance on the Macro Level: Productivity

Performance is another complex term with many meanings that are hard to specify in crisp definitions. One reason it is complex is that it refers to something about the behavior or output of a wide range of entities or systems, ranging from the national economy to the particular work organization, to work groups or teams, and to the individual worker.

On the level of the national economy we are likely to equate good performance with *productivity*. If the ratio of produced goods and services to the costs paid to produce them is high, we usually say the economy is performing well. On this macro level of analysis we generally leave the study of performance and production to the economists. We let them compute their ratios reflecting various productivities of the different factors of production.

The classical economists, of whom Adam Smith is the most famous, saw three categories of such factors: land, capital, and labor. The economists thus compute ratios like the number of tons of soybeans produced per acre per year, the number of dollars in revenue produced for each dollar invested, the number of cars produced per worker-day. All of these indices or statistics reflect varying degrees of performance or productivity.

The economic forces at work have changed since Smith's time 200 years or so ago, and today *technology* and the *methods of allocating resources,* both constituting a broader factor called knowledge, are paramount factors of production. Both land and resources on one hand, and money invested in productive equipment, are considered to constitute *capital.* Thus, taking *labor* into consideration, Campbell McConnell (1984) sees productivity (i.e., the performance of the national economy) affected by four factors.

These four factors interact with each other. For example, to exploit new energy-saving technology harnessing the energy of the sun requires the investment of funds in research and development and in equipment; on the other hand, technology increases the productivity of invested dollars. Investing capital in technology that serves as the tools of labor is the interaction usually of greatest interest. Labor or human resources, the productive factor with which this book is primarily concerned, thus still play an important role.

On the level of the particular work organization, the picture becomes clearer because the resolution level is higher. At this level, practical interventions may produce predictable (short-term) results; hence it is productivity on this level that is usually of greatest interest. As Peter Drucker points out: ". . . what matters in the end is the total, overall productivity of a specific institution in using its resources. What matters is the total overall productivity of this factory, this store, this bank, this hospital, this school, this office" (1980, 28).

This emphasis on the performance of the work organization reflects basically a systems approach to work, an approach that recognizes that it is relatively pointless to condemn individual workers for being unproductive, when they can be productive only under certain necessary conditions which must be provided by their work environment and, specifically, their work organization. Industrial psychologists are increasingly interested in the "systems concept": Their "intent is to develop a 'system' that provides an optimum blend of people, equipment, procedures, and operations in order to capitalize on the relative capabilities of human beings and of physical equipment in performing different functions" (McCormick and Ilgen, 1980, 7).

This systems approach recognizes that the failure of one element in the productive process can stop all output. The parts supplier must deliver before the assembly line plant runs out of any of the parts in its inventory; the nurse must sterilize the scalpels before the operation; the aircraft mechanic must go through his entire checklist if the safety record of the airline is to be maintained in the long run. Of course, fail-safe mechanisms and back-up systems can be developed. They are a mixed blessing, however. While they can avoid disastrous slowdowns and breakdowns of the system, they can be expensive and lead to carelessness.

The performance of a system refers to more than its productivity. In addition to productivity the systems approach also considers maintenance of the system. Berrien (1976) points out that the outputs of systems can be categorized into two classes: formal achievement and need satisfaction outputs. The latter feed back into the system and promote its stability, its long-term effectiveness, and its ability to keep on producing in the future. Very often a manager must decide whether to crash a job and pay a high price in terms of low staff morale, worn-out equipment, and so forth, or whether to progress more slowly, lose a contract or two, face a few displeased shareholders. Japanese managers are said to emphasize maintenance and performance about equally, while Americans are said to be rather single-mindedly productivity-, results-, and formal-achievement-oriented.

Performance on the Micro Level: Individual Performance

To some extent performance and productivity on the macro levels of the national economy and the work organization are aggregates of performances of many individual workers. By examining performance on the micro level of the individual, a more specific understanding of performance can be gained. Individual performances constitute the trees that make up the forest of higher level productivity.

This brings us back to the basic formula underlying the structure of this book. The variant of the formula most relevant here is:

$$\text{Performance} = \text{Competence} \times \text{Work Environment}$$

This formula states a relationship between three constructs. These constructs are not observable; they are concepts or ideas which have been constructed by scientists to help structure and explain the chaotic and confusing empirical world around us. In a sense, as psychologist Jane Loevinger points out, "constructs exist [only] in the minds and magazines of . . . [scientists]" (1957, 642).

The reader may recall Clark Hull from the discussion of learning. One of his important contributions to psychology was his insistence that constructs are useful in spite of the fact that they cannot be observed, provided they are anchored or linked to observable variables. Promising constructs are those that can be inferred from measurable aspects of the person, the environment, and behavior.

This notion of constructs anchored in observable variables, particularly in response variables, points out an important difference between performance and competence. Performance can be regarded as a construct. Looked at in this way, it is a lower level construct than competence. It is closer to the world of observables. But performance can also be thought of as the set of response variables in which competence is anchored. That would make it a cluster of variables from which competence can be inferred or in which competence manifests itself in concrete form.

If we regard performance as a construct, the question arises: Which are the best, the most useful, observable variables from which to infer high or low performance? We can ask the same question in more Hullian terms: To which observable and measurable variables should one consider performance to be anchored? This raises the issue of criterion development, the main topic of this chapter.

DEFINING INDIVIDUAL PERFORMANCE

The focus of this chapter is on measures of performance—more specifically, on measures of individual performance. Measures of performance are said to be criterion measures. They are "way[s] of describing success" (Landy, 1985, 148), "predicted measure[s] for judging the effectiveness of persons, organizations, treatments, or predictors of behavior, results, and organizational effectiveness" (Smith, 1976, 745). Note that these definitions do not distinguish between measuring instrument, test, or scale and the more-elusive criteria that we are really interested in. Criterion measures may predict effectiveness or they may be predicted measures of effectiveness. In either case, they reflect what might be called the first-order bottom line, the matter of immediate interest to most managers and many employees.

Approaches to Defining Performance

In order to develop criterion measures, we need at least a rudimentary definition of *performance*. As in the case of competence, we can start with an ostensive definition, that is, a definition of performance which consists of pointing to examples of it. By pointing to the activities of an Olympic medal winner, a hard-working manager who has increased the output of his department, or a student who obtained high grades and by saying "these are examples of performance," we can convey some idea of what the term means to us.

The next step is a working definition. We might use as our working definition the statement "Performance on production jobs is the quantity of items produced that meet quality specifications, and performance on nonproduction jobs is the number of units and the quality of service rendered." This definition would not get us very far, but it is a starting point based on the distinction between production and nonproduction jobs offered by Maier and Verser (1982). It provides an inkling of the problems raised by performance evaluation. It is much more difficult to evaluate the performance of employees in nonproduction jobs—that is, jobs in which variables other than the quantity of goods and services produced matter—than it is to evaluate the performance of employees in production jobs.

The next level is that of operational definition. We can say "performance is what the supervisor's rating scale measures" or "performance is reflected by a low absenteeism rate." This is the type of definition scientists rely on; they feel comfortable with things that they can measure. An operational definition is one that specifies the operations one must perform to measure something. Of course, the trick is to establish the degree to which measures are valid, that is, the degree to which they measure what they are supposed to measure. If the supervisor's rating scale was drafted on a napkin during lunch it will yield numerical ratings, but it may not measure performance at all.

The highest level of definition is the conceptual one: a verbal definition of performance based on some understanding of what determines it, how it can be measured, and what its consequences are. This requires a theoretical framework of which the construct of performance is a part. Such a framework would have to be more detailed than the general proposition that performance is a function of the interaction of person and environment.

Uses of Criterion Measures

The stage we appear to have reached in the case of performance is that of operational definition. There are a number of reasons that make good operational definitions (measures or criteria of performance) important. They are mainly required in personnel research, in program evaluation, and in performance appraisal.

In personnel research, criteria are used to identify useful tests for predicting successful performance on the job or in training programs. The test constructor's task is to develop a cheap and quick psychological test that measures a criterion on which it is difficult and expensive to collect information. The task may be to predict performance in the cockpit of a Boeing 747. One way to measure the criterion is to let prospective pilots fly it. This could be expensive if they are not very good at it. A better way is to develop psychological tests of spatial and mechanical ability, of motor skills, and so forth, which are related to how well a person flies a large aircraft.

In test construction it is, of course, necessary to have a sample for which both test scores and criterion scores are available. But if the correlation between the two is large enough, the test scores can be used to predict criterion scores of future employees. Costs of developing valid tests must be balanced against the benefit of more accurate selection.

The distinction between psychological test and criterion performance is not always as clear-cut as it is in test construction. The broad way in which criterion measures are defined in industrial and organizational psychology allows for the possibility that good psychological tests can themselves be treated as criteria. Rather than a means to an end, they become an end in themselves. That happens when the effectiveness of training programs is judged in terms of test scores. Beyond that, criterion measures can also play the role of psychological tests or predictors. We may, for example, predict future performance from past performance.

In personnel research we also need criterion measures of performance to develop decision rules used to select the most suitable applicants for jobs. Valid psychological tests are helpful tools, but even given such measures we need to establish cutoff points. Those who score on one side of the cutoff point are accepted; those on the other side are rejected. The optimal cutoff point maximizes hits (suitable applicants selected, unsuitable applicants rejected) and minimizes misses (suitable applicants rejected, unsuitable applicants selected).

To identify hits and misses, and hence the cutoff point, we again need both test scores and criterion scores for an initial sample of respondents. Often more than one predictor variable is involved. This can lead to complex situations. Some criteria are compensatory (we may hire office workers who are either very good keyboarders *or* very good bookkeepers); others are not (we want pilots who have excellent eyesight *and* quick reflexes).

Criterion measures of performance are also used in program evaluation. Training programs, for example, involve the identification of training needs and the development of training objectives. Once the programs are in operation, it is necessary to evaluate their effectiveness. Presumably, they are effective if the trainees score higher on various performance measures.

Finally, criterion measures are applied in the context of performance appraisal. Here the evaluation is concerned with individual employees rather than programs. We need criterion measures to develop performance standards, to provide feedback to employees, and for administrative personnel decision making. Performance appraisal seems to yield more measures of individual performance than any other activity; that is, it may be the most fertile source of operational definitions of the construct.

DIRECT MEASURES OF PERFORMANCE

The distinction between performance and work behavior other than performance has been referred to earlier. Work behavior other than performance includes being absent, quitting the job, accident-producing behavior, and being late. It is indirectly related to performance because it interferes with it.

The direct measures of performance are simply those that attempt to assess performance rather than work behavior other than performance. They are of two kinds: observations of behavior and performance ratings.

Behavioral Indices of Performance

In the final analysis, inferences about human beings are based on their behavior. Observations of behavior thus are not only one type of performance measure, they are the basis of other types as well, in particular judgmental performance ratings and some personnel data used in performance appraisals. The other types of performance measures refer to results of behavior rather than to behavior itself. It is often forgotten that these results are one step removed from observables, that they are inferred, that they are somewhat abstract. Patricia Smith (1976) and others criticize for this reason the relatively low emphasis on behavioral indices of performance.

They are not totally neglected, however. We have already encountered in passing two complex behavioral procedures to measure performance: The in-basket assessment procedure and the assessment center evaluation—in which a wide range of methods are combined—are not only measures of ability, they are clearly also measures of performance.

The behavioral indices can be illustrated by the Behavioral Observation Scales (Latham and Wexley, 1977) which consist of items referring to specific behaviors. Two hypothetical examples of a scale used to assess managerial performance might be the following: "considers the opinions of his/her subordinates" and "responds to request for information within 48 hours." The rater might be asked to respond on a scale ranging from *almost never* to *almost always*.

Judgmental Measures of Performance

Performance ratings of the worker made by supervisors, peers, subordinates, and the worker him- or herself constitute the second direct type of performance indices. They are direct in the sense that they reflect performance rather than other work behavior that may or may not interfere with performance. In the terms of Smith (1976), these measures reflect results rather than behavior and they yield soft (subjective) data.

They are results of behavior or of the observation of behavior. We infer them from the observable, behavioral evidence. They include higher level (more abstract) characteristics like judgment, dependability, leadership, and job knowledge. Measuring such characteristics raises new problems, particularly when their softness makes them subject to a particularly large number of sources of error.

We can rate the degree to which an employee exhibits a particular attribute related to performance. For example, we can rate job knowledge on the scale:

Good

Above Average

Average

Below Average

Poor

We can compare employees (or the performance of employees) on the basis of different attributes. The simplest way to achieve this is to rank order the employees: The employee who exhibits most clearly some desirable attribute like dependability is assigned a rank of 1, and so forth.

The problem with rank ordering is that it can become unsystematic and hence very subjective when more than just a few employees have to be ranked. But there are other methods for comparing employees. The paired comparison method, for example, requires that each possible pair of employees be compared separately. Relatively simple discriminations are made in a systematic way; subjectivity and "snap judgments" may thus be reduced. The judgments might take the form of:

A is more dependable than B

B is more dependable than C

A is more dependable than C

It can happen, of course, that inconsistent judgments are made. For example, if the last of the three judgments above were "C is more dependable than A," our eyebrows would go up. They need not do so unduly, however, since human judgment must be expected to reflect some error and since this method at least allows us to detect inconsistencies. One way to remedy the problem is to use several judges.

Among the various sources of error to which such rating scales are subject there is the well-known *halo effect*, the "tendency to rate an individual either high or low on many factors because the rater knows (or thinks) the individual to be high or low on some specific factor" (McCormick and Ilgen, 1980, 77). Most adults can recall a situation in school where some teacher consistently gave them high or, more likely, low grades on all assignments, regardless of markedly different performances turned in.

While the halo effect depends on the particular person being judged, constant errors, such as the tendency to be lenient or the tendency to rate everyone as average, affect the entire group of employees under review. These constant errors may reflect fairly stable aspects of the rater. Lenient judgments may be an indication that raters want to avoid trouble, do not want to play God with the fate of employees or are hedging their bets because of a lack of confidence and unwillingness to assume responsibility for making definite judgments and accusing others of incompetence. The tendency to rate everyone as average may also indicate a lack of self-confidence. In addition, it may reflect a lack of interest in or laxness about the rating process. There are, of course, also raters who go to extremes. Like Maccoby's (1976) jungle fighters, they may slash at the deadwood with extremely low ratings. Hidden agendas on the part of the raters may have to be considered.

Finally, there are stereotypes that affect the ratings, usually in the downward direction, given to members of particular groups, in particular groups based on race, ethnic origin, and sex.

INDIRECT INDICES OF PERFORMANCE

Organizational records yield a number of "hard" indices that reflect performance indirectly. These fall largely into two categories: those pertaining to work behavior other than performance, such as absenteeism, and those pertaining to the productivity of the individual worker.

Indices of Work Behavior Other Than Performance

While such behaviors as absences, disruption, and quitting often affect judgmental measures of performance (for example, via the halo effect), they are much more clearly reflected in hard rather than subjective personnel data. Such behaviors are of interest in assessing performance because they frequently affect it in a dramatic way. They usually consist of concrete incidents that are recorded in personnel files. The personnel data pertaining to them are, again in the terms of Smith (1976), results inferred from behavior rather than behaviors, but unlike the judgmental indices, they are hard data based on organizational records. However, while they may be more objective than performance ratings, they raise a number of problems of their own.

The most serious problem may be that they are available in meaningful quantity only for a minority of workers: the worst and the best. This means that the indices show so little variability that it is difficult to correlate them with other measures. At best they allow us to identify extremes of performance.

Such data can also be misleading. For example, they make the steady and punctual plodder look better than he should, and they overlook the possibility that the employee who shows up only three days a week is actually producing more than the one who is on the job faithfully but ineffectually every morning at 7:00 A.M. There is a tendency to forget that these indirect indicators are sometimes determinants and sometimes consequences of performance rather than indices of performance as such.

Finally, some of these indices are a scientist's nightmare. For example, there are different kinds of absences. Being absent may reflect low job satisfaction or serious illness that has nothing to do with attitude toward the job. It may occur frequently for short periods in the case of the single parent who has to be at home when the baby sitter is unavailable, or infrequently for long periods in the case of the moonlighter who does occasional jobs out of town. Absences as such do not constitute a single measure or dimension; they form a heterogeneous domain of apples and oranges.

Indices of Individual Productivity

From the point of view of business, performance basically refers to the quantity and quality of a worker's output. Its simplest indicators are the number of items produced and the quality of these items. For example, workers might be evaluated and paid in terms of the number of integrated circuit chips produced that meet quality control standards.

However, while performance and productivity are closely related on the macro level of the organization and the national economy, they turn out to be quite distinct when examined under higher resolution on the micro level of the individual. Indices of individual productivity depend largely on the work environment and they are at best indirect indices of performance. We are again dealing with results—this time not only in Smith's sense of something inferred from behavior, but also in the sense of something that is a salable product of behavior. For a particular job a variety of indices of individual productivity can be constructed or defined. Some of these will be useful for other jobs as well; some will be job-specific. Just because there is a plethora of indices or potential indices, however, does not mean they do not raise their own difficulties.

Productivity indices can be difficult to interpret because they sometimes reflect the influence of the environment and at other times the contribution of the worker. More than behavioral indices, judgmental indices, and personnel data, productivity indices reflect the output of a system that includes more than one worker. Teams, subcontractors who may or may not supply parts, and supervisors who may or may not be knowledgeable are involved in producing this output.

A second problem raised by productivity indices is that their direct relationship to the manager's concerns about the enterprise's productivity can cause them to be overemphasized. The resulting imbalance between concerns for short-term performance and for maintaining the organization and preserving its resources is common. As noted earlier, it is also one that is more characteristic of American than of Japanese firms.

USING PERFORMANCE APPRAISALS TO IMPROVE PERFORMANCE

One reason that explains why performance appraisal has generated interest in operational definitions of performance is that it has the potential for improving individual performance. The manner in which management conducts performance evaluations and discusses the results with employees influences the extent to which that potential is realized.

The feedback aspect of performance evaluation is particularly important because employees, being human, react defensively to criticism. Employees do not relish being told about their weaknesses. They are more likely than their supervisors to emphasize the obstacles they have to contend with. If they are told about their weak points, they are not necessarily going to do anything about them or they may respond in various undesirable ways. For example, the secretary who is told that she is not punctual may resentfully become extremely punctual, to the extent that she will leave the office in mid-sentence at exactly 4:30.

The defensive attitude of employees is often warranted. Maier and Verser point out that "even if an employee has five strong points and only two weaknesses, more interview time will be spent on the weaknesses" (1982, 381). Employees, being human, prefer to hear praise. Managers prefer to work on deficiencies.

Not only are there different needs to be met by the two sides, but the situation under discussion is viewed in quite different ways. Disagreement between managers and employees concerning job duties might be expected to be minimal, but it is not. The chasm that separates the perception of the two sides on the obstacles faced by the employee can be downright unbridgeable.

It seems clear that usually little is achieved by confronting employees with criticism. One way around the problem, requiring great skill on the part of the supervisor, is to engage in meaningful dialogue instead of providing one-way feedback. It must not be fake dialogue; the supervisor must approach the performance appraisal with an open mind and be receptive to the employee's perception of what the obstacles, beyond his or her control, to better performance are. Ideally it is the employee who should formulate the points on which improvement is called for, and these points should be viewed as weak only in relation to strong points.

Much remains to be done in developing or identifying, and in validating, criterion measures. What is needed ultimately are measures yielding results that can be compared across organizations and departments, as well as across occupational groups. This is a tall order because performance assumes different forms for such different groups as blue collar workers and knowledge workers. However, more adequate criterion measures are required if progress is to be made toward satisfactory conceptual definitions of performance. Eventually we may have more than a plethora of more-or-less-valid operational definitions. We may end up with a conceptual definition that will allow us to compare the worth of the work of a particular brick layer and a particular neurosurgeon, so we will no longer automatically assume that whatever the latter does is worth infinitely more than the effort and expertise of the former.

10.
Matching People and Jobs

Proper matching of people and jobs is a critical step in optimizing work performance, productivity, and work satisfaction. This task can be approached in two very different ways (Chapanis, 1976; Mankin, 1978): One can fit people to jobs or one can fit jobs to people.

In the past, certain jobs simply had to be done: the chores on the farm, shoveling coal in the steel plant, hunting the reindeer, weaving the baskets. The job was a given; people were selected who fitted the job, who had the muscle and the intellectual skills to do it. But modern technology has changed that. It is now possible to design jobs so that they can be done with less physical effort and by the handicapped. It is possible to assign monotonous drudgery to machines and computers, and thus to free workers for more interesting activities. In short, the tendency has been to fit people to jobs but it is now possible to fit jobs to people.

As usual, the process of fitting people and jobs can be studied by focusing on people, on the environment, and on the interaction between the two. We can look at people closely to determine what they bring to the job; we can study the cohort graduating from schools and training programs or assess the qualifications of specific job applicants. On the other hand, one can look at the demand for abilities and skills generated by the changing techno-economic structure or, on the level of the individual, at the requirements of a particular job.

Of course, while emphasis on person or environment is possible, matching people and jobs intrinsically concerns the interaction between the two. The relationship between workers and jobs is a very dynamic one. Jobs affect workers and workers affect jobs. There are those who believe that the job can transform recalcitrant citizens into model citizens of a new socialist or free-enterprise order, that it can transform the undisciplined lout into a mature worker with "character," and that it can be a means to growth and understanding.

A second dichotomy used in earlier sections to categorize findings or events under consideration is useful here: that between macro level and micro level analysis. In the preceding chapter on performance, it seemed convenient to draw the line between the two levels so that the national economy as well as the work organization constituted the macro level. In the present context it is useful to include only the former on the macro level. On the micro level we thus have the specific work organization and the individual.

Supply-and-demand questions which concern the national workforce, the values of this workforce, and the educational system that shapes it are here considered to be macro level issues. On the other hand, what one can regard as micro level issues are involved in the assessment of the abilities of workers by a personnel department and in the design of jobs within a particular work organization.

In analyzing the match between people and jobs, competence plays an important role. Both the motivation and the abilities that people bring to the job, or which jobs require, are important. This chapter thus ties together earlier chapters. From the people side, questions arise about assessing motivational dispositions, abilities, and skills and about how to train workers so they exhibit the required motivation and ability. From the job side, the questions of interest raised primarily concern job design.

THE PEOPLE/JOB MATCH ON THE NATIONAL LEVEL

The Three Mismatches of Concern

On the macro level, there are three basic mismatches of concern. All of these have a great deal to do with what sort of jobs one projects for the future. Opinions differ somewhat on this point. Some say that automation will usher in an age of leisure. Others say that the vast majority of people will work in poorly paid jobs requiring next to no skills in the fast food or security areas. Still others project a great need for sophisticated programmers, systems analysts, and electronics engineers.

The first mismatch is that between the number of people who want to work and the number of jobs available. Technology is killing jobs, especially in the manufacturing sector (the "smokestack" industries). The productivity problem is solved as far as "production jobs" (Maier & Verser, 1982) are concerned. It seems doubtful that the workers displaced by robots and microprocessors in the manufacturing sector will all find jobs in the service sector. It also seems doubtful that the computer and other high-technology industries can create a sufficiently large number of jobs to meet the demand for them.

A second mismatch exists between overeducated Americans and the supply of jobs requiring a college education. Good graduates of professional schools will probably always be in demand, in spite of temporary discrepancies between supply of graduates and demand for them. The more serious problem is the situation of college graduates, some with Ph.D.s, who have not specialized in an area deemed useful by the business world. While it is wrong to assume that all college graduates are educated, it is nevertheless the case that there are many college graduates looking for work that will allow them to apply sophisticated knowledge and complex abilities. These are potentially the overeducated Americans that Richard Freeman (1976) and Ivar Berg (1971) have written about.

Finally, there appears to be a mismatch between the number of highly trained Americans and the number of jobs that require a high level of, and a large number of, vocational skills. Here we run into the undertrained rather than the overeducated American. Equalitarian America has neglected vocational training; everyone was told to go to the university and become a college graduate or a professional. One factor shaping this problem has been the idea that everyone is basically the same as everyone else—not just of equal worth, but basically the same. As a result there are far fewer highly trained workers in America than in Japan or Germany. Lawyers seem to be a dime a dozen, while competent plumbers are as hard to find and as treasured as the holy grail.

Upgrading People and Jobs

These three apparent mismatches raise questions that are likely to occupy governments, business, and the job-seeking public for years to come: (1) Will there be enough jobs? (2) Are Americans overeducated? (3) Are Americans undertrained?

The most serious mismatch appears to be the first one. High technology replaces workers at the same time that concerns about unreliable and costly human workers speed up efforts to develop and deploy it. Considerable hope is placed currently in the enterprising nature of individuals unfettered by government regulation. The internally controlled tell the multitude: ''I worked hard and made it. You can too.'' In the absence of eager employers willing to pay high wages, many people are indeed likely to set up small businesses themselves.

Work in the future may not assume the traditional form of the *job*. Most workers today are employees who occupy a fairly fixed niche in the structure of the work organization. A certain stability and predictability are associated with these niches. In the future there may be fewer such niches, and more people may be entrepreneurs running their own small operation providing some service or product. More people may be ''intrapreneurs'' (Pinchot, 1985) who work for a particular corporation and on a project basis rather than a fixed 40-hour work week. Rapid technological change may not only make the regular work week, but also the notions of *occupation* and *vocation,* obsolete. What is left is the person-centered notion of *career*, the useful tasks for which there is both a need and a demand, which one has done in the past and which one presumably is able to do in the future.

The remaining two mismatches, involving overeducated and undertrained workers, are related. Those who look down on blue-collar work are those who think everyone should go to college; a shortage of craftsmen and repairmen goes hand in hand with a glut of semi-literate university graduates.

In theory the schools can be changed to meet the demands of the workplace or the workplace can be changed to accommodate the graduates of the schools. The economists, whom O'Toole (1977, 114) calls the "human capitalists," tend to adopt the first of these strategies. They see the problem as one of overeducation. Freeman (1976), for example, argues that the remedy to the imbalance between abilities and jobs is to train fewer people at the college level since such training pays off no longer either for the individual who will end up with a routine job anyway or for the society of which the disappointed "overeducated" individual will not be a particularly enthusiastic and productive member.

The economists would advocate the teaching of more Business English and less Old English Literature. In general, students and parents tend to adopt this position and to keep their eyes on changes in demand. When word spreads that there is a surplus of schoolteachers, enrollment in the faculties of art drops. When the business community goes all out to hire formally trained future decision makers, the multitudes knock on the doors of the business faculties.

The educators—O'Toole's "humanists"—would like to change the nature of jobs. They are inclined to say to the business sector: "Look at the competent problem solvers we have nurtured. Kindly provide jobs that allow them to use their talents." Business, of course, falls off the chair laughing. The educators see the problem as one of underemployment, not overeducation. They think that the bankers should hire tellers who can add and subtract, and that police departments should employ applicants with degrees in social work.

The reason the argument between the human capitalists and the humanists is a protracted one is that both sides make an important point. As the human capitalists note, the demand for labor is *the* critical variable. However, the humanists are right in maintaining that upgrading jobs by means of job enrichment (discussed later in this chapter) and upgrading the qualifications of the workforce through greater investment in training and more rigorous education are both also necessary to deal with mismatches between the qualifications of job seekers and the demands of available jobs.

FITTING THE PERSON TO THE JOB:
PERSONNEL SELECTION AND TRAINING

The problem in fitting persons to jobs is to select from the available candidates, within and outside the organization, those who can do a given set of jobs best. It is not just a matter of finding the best person for the job. Sometimes the best people are already working for the organization and are more effective in their present jobs than they would be in new ones. In other cases, the best person filling a new job may keep another employee out of it who, while second best, might be much more effective in the new job than the old one. The problem is one of matching people and jobs so that the joint performance of all employees in all jobs will be maximized.

The objective of optimal deployment of human resources is attained by a variety of personnel actions or personnel decisions. Some of these decisions involve the hiring of new employees. Given the results of formal or informal job analyses, job specifications, and human resource planning designed to provide a picture of what types of new employees are needed, the firm will typically proceed to recruit applicants by advertising. The next step is usually to select from a large number of applicants those who best meet the requirements of a smaller number of jobs to be filled.

These selection decisions are based on interpersonal differences. Applicants are compared with each other and those scoring highest on desirable criteria are accepted. At this point, intrapersonal differences are usually looked at more closely. The particular strengths and weaknesses of applicants are considered as placement or classification decisions are made, that is, as the applicants are assigned to particular training programs or jobs.

A closer look at the placement process shows that the distinctions between the different types of personnel decisions are quite fuzzy. As Wayne Cascio (1982) points out, in practice people are selected for specific job categories or for specific jobs. This means that selection usually already involves placement and classification decisions. While the latter are often distinct processes involving people who have already been selected or hired, selection goes hand in hand with them, that is, with decisions about how to treat successful applicants, or what job or training to assign them to.

A second area of fuzziness is the distinction between placement and classification. Anne Anastasi (1982) makes a clear distinction between placement as a process that involves one criterion (a single dimension of ability or motivational disposition such as intelligence or interest in working with numbers) and classification as one that involves two or more criteria. In practice the distinction is not maintained. (See Cascio, 1982, and Landy, 1985).

For present purposes what seems important is that classification is the more general process—the process of assigning people to a variety of jobs differing in two or more job specifications. It is also apparent that both selection and placement are not only personnel decisions pertaining to the hiring of new employees, but that they also underlie other personnel decisions such as promotion or reclassification.

Other personnel actions involve the redeployment of personnel within a particular work organization. Among these the most prominent are promoting, transferring, or demoting employees. Finally there are personnel actions focusing on removing present employees. These include retiring people and, more painfully, firing (de-hiring, or terminating) them.

Identifying Job Requirements

Most, perhaps all, of the personnel decisions listed above require a knowledge of what abilities and other person characteristics are demanded by particular jobs. Job analysis tells us what jobs consist of, what tasks they put before the worker, and what activities the worker must engage in. The next step in fitting people to jobs is to determine what motivational dispositions and what knowledge, abilities, and skills the jobs call for. These job requirements are also called job specifications or personnel specifications.

Valid job requirements are intrinsic in the job: general aptitudes or sensory and physical abilities. A bookkeeper's job requires numerical abilities; a warehouse loader's job requires strength and endurance. Jobs also intrinsically require specific skills and knowledge: an understanding of ledgers or the ability to drive a forklift truck. Equal employment legislation requires that only those variables that are correlated with job performance be considered in the selection of personnel. Such correlation and hence relevance may be difficult to establish in the case of extrinsic job requirements pertaining to sex, marital status, age, race, and so forth. It thus has become more difficult to impose unfounded preferences (prejudices) in the selection and placement of workers.

McCormick and Ilgen (1985) discuss three main methods for establishing job requirements. These methods assume that a job analysis has been done, that it is known what the job elements or job components are.

First, there are methods based on judgment. These methods underlie the U.S. Training and Employment Service method for specifying "worker trait requirements" for jobs listed in the U.S. government's official list of jobs, the *Dictionary of Occupational Titles* (U.S. Department of Labor, 1977). Job analysts infer from the identified job elements or job components what levels of general intelligence, verbal or numerical skills, motor coordination, and so forth are required.

Second, there are methods based on structured job analyses. In this generally more formal approach the questions raised are: (1) What are the job dimensions (groups of job elements)? (2) How important is each? (3)

What traits and abilities are required? (4) What methods (e.g., psychological tests) are available for identifying the required abilities and motivational dispositions?

Finally, there are methods based on statistical analysis. McCormick and Ilgen (1985) cite a study by Fleishman and Berniger (1960) to illustrate this approach. The objective of the study was to find predictors of job tenure (the criterion). Long job tenure (defined as holding the job for more than two years) was deemed desirable. The question was, Which types of employees are likely to remain on the job for a while?

Fleishman and Berniger began by obtaining data from a derivation sample of 120 female office workers hired in the course of a two-year period. They divided the sample into a long-tenure group that had stayed on the job for two years or more, and a short-tenure group that had left after less than two years. To illustrate their findings: One variable that differentiated between the two groups and that had potential as a predictor of job tenure was age. For example, the percentage of workers younger than 20 years old in each group was 8 and 35, respectively; for workers older than 35 years it was 48 and 11. Fleishman and Berniger assigned weights of -3 and $+3$ to these two age categories. In other words, older workers were deemed much more likely to stay on the job. Note that no predicting has taken place yet. To derive a prediction equation or prediction weights you need a derivation sample for which both the predictor and criterion information are available. Only when you have established the prediction equation or the prediction weights do you try to predict.

To predict, you need a second sample. Since this second sample is used to test the prediction weights, it is called the validation sample. Fleishman and Berniger selected a second sample of 85 persons hired during the same period. Using age and other predictors they found that of those new subjects who obtained a weighted predictor score above a certain level, 68% had stayed for two years or more, and of those who obtained a score below that level, only 22% had stayed that long. This indicates that useful predictors were identified which could permit the selection of new personnel who would stay on, thus reducing training costs and perhaps improving productivity.

Identifying Worker Characteristics

While interviews and biographical information are useful in identifying worker characteristics that may, or may not, match the requirements of jobs to be filled, it is psychological tests that are the more standardized, quantitative, and reliable sources of information on psychological worker characteristics. These tests measure personality traits (e.g., the Personality Research Form [Jackson, 1974] and the Sixteen Personality Factor Questionnaire [Cattell, Eber, and Tatsuoka, 1970]); interests (e.g., the

Jackson Vocational Interest Blank [Jackson, 1982], the Strong-Campbell Interest Inventory [Campbell, 1977], and the Kuder Occupational Interest Survey [Kuder, 1979]; and abilities and skills, including a variety of intelligence tests and more specific measures of vocational abilities like the Bennett Mechanical Comprehension Test (1969).

An important feature of psychological tests is that their validity, the degree to which they measure what they are supposed to measure, can be assessed.

Tests may be supposed to measure abilities or personality traits that are expected to manifest themselves in correct responses made to sets of algebraic or accounting problems. When we have items whose responses can be said to reflect the presence or absence of the characteristic we are interested in, the test has content validity. This is admittedly a somewhat subjective type of validity.

A more ambitious type is criterion validity. Tests may be supposed to measure certain criterion measures, such as a supervisor's rating of job performance or the number of insurance policies sold. If the test has a high correlation with some criterion measure, it is said to have criterion validity.

Finally, a test may be supposed to measure certain constructs, such as initiative or independence. These constructs differ from criteria in a clear-cut way. They are not directly measurable; they are inferred rather than observable; there are no criterion measures available. This means that establishing construct validity is a long-term research effort in which many hypotheses are tested until one can infer that the test indeed measures the indirectly accessible construct.

There are thus three types of validity: content, criterion, and construct. The last is the most important because it embraces the other two. Content and criterion validity are among the indicators of construct validity. Construct validity is also important because the underlying constructs embedded in scientific theories have second-order relevance and are more general and stable than observable variables.

Relating Measures of Worker Characteristics to Job Components

Even the most valid tests are not good enough. As noted, equal employment legislation requires that employers demonstrate that the predictors they use in selecting employees are valid for the specific purpose they are supposed to serve. While a test that measures verbal fluency is very interesting, it may be irrelevant for selecting people to drive locomotives or maintain dry-cleaning equipment. The point is that evidence must be available that links psychological tests and other predictors to the jobs that are to be filled.

This raises a problem. In applied situations like personnel selection, the most convincing type of validity is predictive criterion validity. But a study demonstrating predictive validity is complex and costly. Not only does it require a large derivation sample from which validity coefficients are obtained that identify the most valid predictors of success on the job, it also requires a test or cross-validation sample to determine the replicability of validity coefficients and hit rates obtained by using the predictors.

For both derivation and test sample the initial predictor scores and final criterion scores have to be obtained. It is difficult to obtain the criterion scores; they become available only after the subjects have been on the job for some time. In addition, all subjects should be hired and then tested at the end of a period of employment, not only the most promising ones. The reason is that validity coefficients are underestimated when they are computed on a selected subsample consisting of only the people obtaining high scores on a predictor. A predictor can be effective only if it differentiates among people, that is, if there are both high and low scorers.

It is unlikely that employers or their personnel departments can prove their tests are valid by going the traditional route of predictive validity. The costs are generally too high. Fortunately there are other ways. One of these involves the concept of job component validity. Unlike the more commonly known types of test validity alluded to above, this fourth type is concerned as much with aspects of the person as with aspects of the environment into which that person is supposed to fit.

The underlying logic is that (1) all jobs involve the same basic set of job components (i.e., the difference between jobs lies in the *degree* to which they involve the same basic job components), and (2) predicting performance on individual job components is more promising than predicting performance on specific jobs because it allows us to make predictions about the whole array of jobs for which a particular job component is important.

The first step in establishing job component validity is to identify the components of jobs. That is the job analyst's function. For example, the job analysts tell us that the PAQ dimension "clerical/related activities" is involved in many jobs, including the job of filing clerk. If we can predict success on this component, we have made a first step toward predicting success in many jobs.

The second step is to identify worker characteristics that are related to performance on various job components. Theoretically there is a difference between worker characteristics and their measures; in practice the latter serve as the operational definitions of the former and are equated with them.

If we assume that people usually find jobs that call for the levels of the abilities that they can bring to the job, then an index like the mean score obtained on relevant tests by job incumbents can tell us what abilities a job calls for (McCormick, Mecham, and Jeanneret, 1977). By correlating the importance of job components of many jobs with the mean ability scores of the job incumbents we can establish the degree of relationship between job components and the measures of ability we plan to use as predictors of performance. McCormick et al., for example, found a high correlation between the Clerical Perception subscale of the General Aptitude Test Battery of the U.S. Employment Service and "clerical/related activities." This finding makes the Clerical Perception subscale a promising predictor for any job that involves "clerical/related activities." (See Appendix 2 for somewhat more detail on the type of statistics computed by McCormick et al.)

A Note on the Role of Training in Matching People and Jobs

Training has been discussed earlier in the chapters on ability. What is of interest here is the potential of training, particularly of employer-sponsored training, to change workers so they will fit a particular job. The desired change may assume different forms: raising ability and skill levels or developing new abilities, skills, and knowledge. In some cases workers may even be expected to learn to ignore abilities and knowledge previously acquired and to suspend their thought processes while working on routine tasks.

If the match between personnel and jobs is not satisfactory, training can change the people that have already been hired, who have seniority, or whose skills may be obsolete. It is hard to fire personnel these days; employees have rights. At least retraining can keep people serving useful purposes longer. Thus where personnel selection provides the human parts that enable the work organization to produce, training provides the lubricant that makes these parts mesh more smoothly with each other and with other elements of the workplace.

FITTING JOBS TO PEOPLE: JOB DESIGN

The expectations of the modern worker are high. There is much less willingness to accept any job and to let oneself be ordered about than 30 or 60 years ago. People are aware of their rights, and the affluent 1970s created the strong impression that it is no longer necessary to work like a mule. More than half of the workforce is said to espouse "new breed" or postindustrial values rather than the old-fashioned industrial values of the Protestant work ethic (Yankelovich, 1979, 1981).

At the same time, technology is making it possible to redesign jobs so that they are less fatiguing and possibly more interesting. Robots can do the physically demanding and unpleasant work; computers can perform the repetitive mental functions and allow the human workforce to get straight to the decision making.

Both the higher expectations of workers and the job-changing potential of technology appear to be contributing to a shift from selecting personnel for fixed slots to changing the slots to fit people.

Job design involves the introduction of systematic changes of aspects of the work environment. Any of the aspects of the work environment listed in Exhibit 8-1 may be modified by the job designer. The independent variables (causes or determinants) of interest may be the work tasks themselves; physical conditions pertaining to the workplace (like illumination); the work schedule (which could be changed by introducing flextime giving the employee a certain freedom to choose when to be on the job); the social environment (which could be changed by hiring a new manager more concerned with maintenance than with performance).

Of these aspects of the work environment the job itself is probably the most important. It is the common core of primary importance no matter what the job may be. This suggests another reason for assigning to job analysis a central role in matching people and jobs and in influencing work performance and work satisfaction.

Work performance and satisfaction are the dependent variables of interest in job design. They are the variables that we attempt to increase. This raises a problem: Increasing performance and increasing work satisfaction appear to be objectives that job designers approach in two contradictory ways. The productivity and job-oriented engineers performed motion and time studies and developed the body of knowledge called human engineering, while the work satisfaction and worker-oriented psychologists stressed human relations and quality-of-working-life programs. Exhibit 10-1 presents some of the major differences between these approaches which are discussed in the next two sections.

Exhibit 10-1
The Two Approaches to Job Design

	Job simplification	Job enrichment
Variables affected:	work performance, productivity	work satisfaction
Variants of job design involved:	methods analysis, human factors engineering	horizontal loading, vertical loading
Aspect of worker addressed:	ability	motivation
Theoretical base:	systems theory	Herzberg's theory, job characteristics model

Decreasing Job Scope: Job Simplification

Originally, the motivation underlying job design efforts was to increase productivity. The earliest well-known efforts were those of Frederick Taylor (1911) and Frank Gilbreth (1911) and they assumed the form of methods analysis. The best way to perform the activities constituting a job was scientifically determined by analyzing the motions of the worker and the time required by them and by applying, for example, the basic laws of mechanics. This approach is still important: The efficiency expert with clipboard in one hand and stopwatch in the other is still a common, though not necessarily popular, sight.

As work began to involve more complex machinery and electronic devices, a broader approach emerged focusing on man-machine systems. This approach led to the development of the discipline of human-factors engineering or ergonomics. Human-factors engineering is described by Alphonse Chapanis as the discipline that is

primarily concerned with the discovery and application of information about human behavior in relation to machines, tools, jobs, and work environments [and whose] ultimate goal . . . is to help in the design of equipment, tasks, work places, and work environments so that they best match worker abilities and limitations. [1976, 698]

An important aspect of human-factors engineering that emerges clearly from this definition is its focus on the abilities rather than the motivation of the worker. The person is assumed to be a given set of abilities—they may be as mundane as being able to comfortably reach switches placed within arm's length—to which the job is to be fitted. The general trend, and this seems to hold for methods analysis as well, is to make things simpler for the worker. This not only benefits the employer, who can expect higher levels of performance and reduced training costs, it also makes life easier for the worker, at least in the short run.

The general framework of human-factors engineering is systems theoretical. It essentially approaches the worker as a machine, or at least a subsystem that is part of the larger productive system (i.e., the team or the combination of worker and work environment characterized primarily by certain equipment, machines, or tools). This subsystem has input, mediating or processing, and output functions.

Input functions. According to F. Kenneth Berrien (1976), there are really two kinds of inputs: signal and maintenance. The latter are of less interest to the job designer than the former, although one might argue that job design could include facilities for eating properly and relaxing between periods of work. In practice, job design is mainly concerned with signal inputs, with the question "How do workers get the information they need to do their jobs?"

The human-factors engineer can design displays that transmit information in an unambiguous way by choosing the most appropriate sensory
modality, using meaningful and easily understood codes, using soothing or
arousing colors, and shaping displays for optimal effect. For example, in a
particular situation the optimal display might be visual (rather than
auditory), it might use a complicated but standard code (letters rather than
patterns of dots or lines). This is the type of display offered by video display
terminals.

Processing functions. These are processes that mediate between input and
output; they constitute the throughput. The job designer may keep two
principles in mind here. The first is that reducing the number of input
signals and output actions makes the work easier. Less decision time is
required. When there are two input signals and two output alternatives
(e.g., two keys on a special keyboard), the response time is about one
second; when there are 100 of each, response time is twice that (Hilgendorf,
1966, cited from McCormick and Ilgen, 1985, 357).

A second principle guiding many job design interventions is that when
input signals and responses are compatible with the worker's expectations,
performance is better (in terms of time, accuracy, and so forth) than when
they are not. McCormick and Ilgen (1985) distinguish among spatial,
movement, and conceptual compatibility. There is spatial compatibility
when the emergency switch is immediately below the dial indicating danger.
There appears to be compatibility of movement when we push the gas pedal
to increase speed and, although in the modern autumble it has become a
vestige, occasionally pull the emergency brake to bring the vehicle to a stop.
Finally, there is conceptual compatibility when danger is indicated by
arousing red signals rather than soothing blue ones.

Output functions. Here we deal with the implementation of decisions.
The focus is on things like the location and design of control devices.
Workers in general are quick and accurate in emergencies when controls are
at shoulder height. Individual differences may be an important consideration here. If all workers have to be able to sound an alarm quickly, the
controls should perhaps be designed for the lowest 20 percent of performers. When errors are particularly costly and must be avoided at almost
any cost, we might design even more forgiving, "idiot-proof" systems for
the "lowest common denominator."

McCormick and Ilgen (1985) point out that the shape of control knobs on
aircraft may suggest the function they control so the pilot can feel whether
the right device is being manipulated, that handwheels should have
diameters between 7 and 21 inches and a maximum displacement between
90 and 120 degrees, and that specially bent cutting pliers used to cut parts
for injection-molded plastic boxes can improve the postures of the workers.

Parenthetically one may note the parallel between the first three
categories of McCormick at al.'s (1977) job elements for the PAQ and these

three categories of functions. Underlying both is the general stimulus-organism-responses (S-O-R) paradigm of behavior. As in the case of the PAQ, the model does not cover every aspect of the work situation of interest. The S-O-R subsystem operates within a work space envelope, in certain facilities, in a certain physical position. How all of these can be affected (optimized) by work design is again illustrated by McCormick and Ilgen (1985). The work space envelope of a seated worker ranges from 45 degrees to the left to 135 degrees to the right; the facilities, not just a particular work station, can be designed so that the emergency controls are within easy reach; the posture of the worker may be improved by means of new types of chairs with inclined seats and pads to support the knees.

Increasing Job Scope: Job Enrichment

The engineer's productivity-oriented approach to job design sees the worker as part of the productive man-machine system. It really neglects the psychological needs of the worker. While it can make the worker's life easier, its immediate effect is often to dehumanize work and to "deskill" the worker.

The new values of many workers—the insistence of the "new breeders" on challenge and growth opportunities—have been one major force bringing about a shift of attention from productivity to work satisfaction. Another factor may be the fact that technology has really solved the productivity problem. There are problems in managing human wants and in distributing the goods produced by the technological horn of plenty, but deep down the people of the industrialized world probably know that they could do without the latest-model refrigerator or the latest-model car with a milkshake dispenser on the dashboard.

Thus there is increasing emphasis on the quality of life and work satisfaction. In some ways this emphasis leads one to design jobs quite differently from the productivity-oriented approaches of methods analysis and human engineering. The objective is to make jobs more complex, challenging, demanding, interesting, and meaningful.

The approaches to job design oriented toward work satisfaction are encompassed by the term *job enlargement*, a term that refers to increasing the number of tasks and the significance of responsibilities associated with a job. There are two kinds of enlargement. Horizontal enlargement refers to increasing the number of tasks included by a job. The cashier collecting money and operating the conveyor belt may also be assigned the task of changing prices on the shelves and perhaps even bagging groceries (union regulations permitting). Job rotation, said to be popular in Japan, can be a reasonably dramatic and formal form of horizontal job enlargement.

The second kind of job enlargement is usually more significant. This is vertical enlargement, also called job enrichment. The emphasis is on increasing the responsibilities, not just the number of tasks, associated with a job. One approach that falls into this category is the introduction of autonomous or semi-autonomous work groups. For example, in the Volvo plant at Kalmar, Sweden, workers form teams that build a car on a movable platform from its beginnings until it is completed. Instead of standing in a fixed position with cars moving past them on an assembly line, the workers follow the platform through the various departments, participate in the different phases of car construction, help make the decisions such a major project requires, and have a chance to see what it is they have been working on.

Job enlargement in general and job enrichment in particular are more concerned with motivation than with ability. Job simplification made managers more happy than it did workers, and job enrichment is in part a corrective measure taken to undo some of the damage of job simplification to the work motivation and morale of many workers.

Its theoretical basis is Herzberg's distinction between motivators intrinsic in the work (ignored by job simplification) and hygienes extrinsic to it. We saw earlier that this theory is interesting but no longer widely accepted. Its role as a basis of job enrichment efforts has in part been taken over by the job characteristics model of Hackman and Oldham (1980). These authors distinguish between jobs with high and low *motivating potential scores* (MPS). The MPS is a function of five variables: the variety of skills required by the job, the degree to which the tasks completed are identifiable, the significance of the work tasks, the degree of autonomy of the worker, and the extent to which feedback is obtained. Job enrichment in the context of this model serves the purpose of raising the MPS of a job.

Maximizing Both Productivity and Work Satisfaction

Fortunately, as the notion of MPS linking work satisfaction and work motivation suggests, the objectives of increasing productivity and work satisfaction (the quality of working life) are not as incompatible as they appear to be at first sight. Methods analysis and human-factors engineering can contribute to work satisfaction by removing onerous, stress-producing, and pointless aspects of the work. Furthermore, by raising productivity they generate wealth which the workers may share and find satisfying. On the other hand, increased work satisfaction, if it is contingent on performance, can reinforce high performance behaviors and raise productivity. Perhaps even more important is the fact that work satisfaction reduces work behavior, such as absenteeism, that can interfere with productivity.

The idea that there can be a close relationship between productivity and work satisfaction underlies and motivates the currently popular quality of working life (QWL) projects under way in many organizations. These programs are more comprehensive than methods analysis and human engineering. Their focus is on the social component of the work situation, that is, on the sociotechnical system of worker and computers, machines, or tools.

The concept of the quality of working life was introduced by Louis Davis around 1972 to refer to a central construct that had evolved out of a number of studies done under the auspices of the Human Resources Centre of the Tavistock Institute in London.

The first of these studies, by Eric Trist and K. W. Bamforth (1951), investigated the introduction of changes in the method of "coal getting" in a British colliery. The ability to construct safer roofs in the mines allowed a return to the "longwall method of goal getting" which required larger work groups and more highly specialized workers. The new technical system was introduced without considering its effects on the workers, that is, the social aspect of the sociotechnical system. The workers responded in unexpected ways; informally they continued to share tasks. Only after a period characterized by culture lag was the social system integrated with the technical system and the emphasis placed on maximizing the output and the work satisfaction produced by the total system.

Einar Thorsrud was instrumental in applying insights obtained at the Tavistock Institute on a large scale in Norway (Emery and Thorsrud, 1969) in the form of the Norwegian Industrial Democracy Project. The Norwegian Confederation of Labor demanded worker representation on boards of directors, and these demands were a symptom of a postwar morale crisis that gripped Norwegian labor relations. There were successful pilot projects involving worker representation and partially autonomous groups in the plants, but their effects were not well received by the prevailing and conservative work culture, and eventually it was Sweden that emerged as the Scandinavian country known for participatory decision making and Germany that emerged as the country pioneering industrial democracy on the industry-wide and national levels.

The QWL concept plays an important role in Japanese management. Davis and Trist (1974) suggest that it has been instrumental in reducing both the traditional prerogatives of seniority and the Taylorism imported after the war. It did so by means of quality control circles and the sempai-kohai relationships between cooperating mentors and protégés. Both of these aspects of Japanese management are part of the bottom-up management style which is generally encouraged by senior management levels in Japan.

In the United States, QWL projects are the rule rather than the exception. This does not mean that progress is rapid and unhampered. There is deep distrust between management and labor. However difficult the implementation of plans to increase the QWL may be, it is of great importance because it is a concrete step toward a major problem facing the workforce of the United States: the gap or even chasm that separates the culture and the techno-economic structure (Bell, 1976). The media-diffused culture tells Americans to focus on self-development and immediate gratification while the workplace demands that they adhere to the rules, regulations, standards, and schedules imposed by work and by managers in the factory and at the office. This conflict reduces the readiness of Americans to put their shoulders to the wheel. Viewed from this perspective, QWL projects are efforts to make working within the techno-economic structure a little more like living within the culture.

RETROSPECT AND PROSPECT

The three chapters constituting this part of the book are closely related. Job analysis lies at the root of most of the topics discussed. Its central role is depicted in Exhibit 10-2. As noted in Chapter 8, job analysis is of particular importance in criterion development (the topic of Chapter 9) and in matching people and jobs (the topic of the present chapter). The domain covered by Exhibit 10-2 is that of matching people and jobs to optimize performance appraised by means of criterion measures. This domain includes the employment process represented in more detail by Cascio (1982, 41).

Exhibit 10-2
The Central Role of Job Analysis

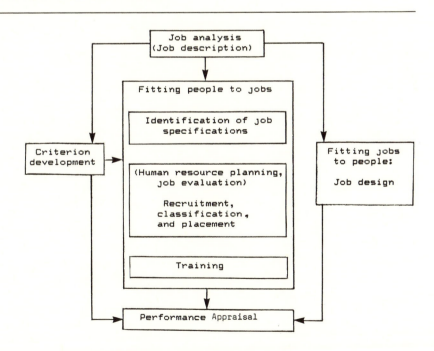

Once job analysis has given us a job description, we can identify indicators of performance on the job. These criteria, these "measures of success," play a direct role in constructing predictors of future performance that are used in personnel selection and related endeavors. However, the main role the criteria play is in the appraisal of employees' performance.

The performance appraised is in part a function of the competence (i.e., the motivation and ability) of the employee. More immediately, since competence is translated into performance only in given work environments, it is a function of the goodness of fit between competent or incompetent worker and the work situation. A large proportion of managing activity deals with assuring good person-job fits by fitting jobs to persons. The outcomes of performance appraisals of employees reflect thus not only the employees' activities, but those of management as well.

PART IV.

QUALITY

11.

The Real Bottom Line

Let's assume that high performance appraisals are obtained, and that many individual performances, reflecting competent workers and good management able to arrange satisfactory person-job matches, add up to a high level of performance and high productivity on the levels of the work organization and the national economy. Is this the end of our concerns? Can we finally relax?

Not really. At this point an often-overlooked question arises. Is high performance a worthy ultimate goal? Is the quest for high performance—for success, for high criterion scores—simply a never-ending rat race associated with ever-higher expectations and ever more consumption which the planet can no longer bear? This is the final question we need to address.

Consider for a moment the following almost laughably implausible situation. The elderly lady has phoned the cab company. The cab arrives, and the elderly lady appears at the door. With the aid of her cane, she slowly begins to negotiate the steps from the apartment building to the street. The alert and courteous driver jumps out of his car, rushes to her side, and helps her to the front seat of his cab.

A small gesture? Perhaps not if the driver is always that alert; not if all drivers of his company have been trained to be of assistance, to resist the impulse of blowing fetid cigar smoke into their passengers' nostrils, to wear something other than ripped jeans and dirty boots, to administer first aid and to generally respond to emergencies. A society whose cab drivers perform their jobs competently offers a higher quality of life than one whose cab drivers may or may not show up, who lose their way, who chew smelly cigar butts, and who see their job as extracting the maximum in return for the minimum.

Of course, there is more to the quality of life than helpful cab drivers. Millions can afford neither taxis nor their own cars in cities whose public transit systems are less reliable than the Pony Express used to be. It will take much more than the best-intentioned and most competent cab drivers to make life more agreeable for the poor, helpless, old, and just plain confused.

Nevertheless, this example throws some light on the most important reason for going to the trouble of working and for doing our work competently. Work is a social activity that affects the quality of life of those around us. By itself that fact may not seem compelling. But if we see ourselves as exchanging our competent work for the benefits produced by the competent work of others, we may see the matter in a new light.

Anthropologist Marvin Harris has pointed out that "if one is sewing a parka for a husband who is about to go hunting for the family with the temperature at sixty below, all stitches will be perfect" (1981, 23). There are fail-safe mechanisms and redundancies in modern societies that make our dependence on the work of others less a matter of life and death than it is among the Inuit. But dependent on the work of others we remain: We hope the butcher knows what he is doing and that we will not eat unsanitary meat, that the doctor diagnoses us correctly, that the traffic policeman will prevent a traffic jam so we can get home without developing an ulcer.

The cab driver example also suggests a second reason for performing work competently: People who do their work well tend to derive much greater satisfaction from it than those who do it in slipshod fashion. Competent drivers are more likely to feel that they play a useful role than their cigar-chomping colleagues who are unwilling to get out of the car. In addition, most people need to feel that they function competently. These higher level or neurogenic needs are satisfied only by competent work.

The bottom line of work is the contribution it makes to the quality of life of the beneficiaries of the work and of the workers themselves. There has been an increasing awareness that the quality of life must be the bottom line of our social concerns and efforts. Technology has generated the level of affluence that allows more than just the privileged few to look beyond immediate bread-and-butter issues. At the same time this affluence is clearly threatened, in part by an overreliance on technology that depletes natural resources at a rapid rate. Not only are we affluent enough to look beyond the problems of bringing home the bacon and providing shelter now and in the immediate future, but we also see clearly, as we look beyond these basic concerns, that bringing home the bacon and providing shelter in the style to which we have become accustomed may be more difficult in the future than it was in the 1960s and 1970s.

Small groups of individuals and particularly lucky communities have, of course, had the time to ponder their quality of life in the past. The citizens of Athens, though probably not the many foreign slaves who kept Greek households humming, discussed happiness and the conditions that made it most probable. The courts of ancient Egypt, Assyria, Persia, and Rome, and the aristocracies of medieval Europe, found time to pursue questions concerning the nature of the good life. But it was only recently, and in the industrialized democracies, that the majority of the population had the opportunity to do more than toil in the fields and beat off the enemy.

APPROACHES TO THE QUALITY OF LIFE

The quality of life is a slippery notion best approached carefully by looking at specific facts that have been established about it. What are the components of the quality of life that have been identified by means of empirical and rational approaches? An understanding of some of its specific components may provide a foundation for some speculative considerations on how they combine to form the elusive whole that we call a high quality of life. These speculations should rely on systems theory, the modern approach to complex wholes. The system or whole of interest consists of individuals and an environment that are in balance, that is, are matched so personal needs are neither nonexistent nor destructively acute and so the environment is able to meet a wide range of legitimate and moderate needs.

An Analytical Approach: Aspects of the Quality of Life

What we need in order to understand intuitively the meaning of "quality of life" are instances we can point to and about which we can say, "That indicates a high quality of life" or "That indicates a low quality of life." In other words, we once again begin with an ostensive definition. The elderly lady encountering a helpful cab driver constitutes a useful instance. A good source of examples of high and low quality of life is an examination of one's own life or that of close acquaintances and the identification of instances, changes, and events that caused us or them to be pleased or displeased with the world and with life. By looking at some specific trees in this fashion we may take the first step toward understanding the general nature of the forest.

When we do that, we must keep in mind that a high quality of life means different things to different people. To the shantytown dweller it means sewers instead of open drains. To workers it may mean work paced by themselves rather than by the relentless conveyor belt. To the deprived child it may mean the occasional pork chop. To the environmentalist it means smokestacks that do not belch black clouds into the air, and to the unemployed worker it means smokestacks that do. To the pensioner it means a postal service that reliably delivers the pension check, government clerks who do more than pass the buck, and bus drivers who know that a 78 year old is not likely to leap off the bus like a teenager.

Of course, we can go beyond descriptive examples. The next step is to formulate categories of incidents or observations that convey a more general understanding of what we mean by "quality of life." Classification is a first step in attaining a scientific understanding of a domain of phenomena or entities. At this point one can proceed by classifying data inductively and empirically, or by classifying them deductively and rationally. Inductively one could extend the examination of critical incidents in one's own life and that of acquaintances and systematically ask a representative sample of citizens what critical incidents or events have increased or decreased their satisfaction with their life. Deductively one could proceed with a rational analysis of how people interact with the environment and examine whether the satisfactions and dissatisfactions that result from this interaction share certain hypothesized features.

The deductive or rational approach starts with a set of hypotheses. The simplest of these concern the nature of categories of events in the domain of interest. Different people may interpret the request to provide critical incidents differently, and inductive grouping of their replies may lead to categories subject to misinterpretation and disagreement. The rational approach seeks to avoid this by starting with hypotheses about the kinds of incidents affecting people's general sense of well-being and it proceeds to look for them. It involves active search, not just passive recording of observations. This active approach may uncover evidence that might escape the passive observer and it may lead to empirical support for a rational framework, a theory, that has explanatory power.

But the rational approach also has its drawbacks. Often the wealth of data produced by thousands of people interacting with thousands of objectively different and differently perceived environments will not fit an elegant rational framework. In the difficulties that ensue, the tendency is to stick to the tidy framework and to ignore the messy data that do not fit it.

The categories yielded by these different approaches may overlap or they may even be the same since they cover the same domain of observations. For example, one common category might consist of incidents pertaining to people's close relationships, and this category might include the incident "son graduates from law school and gratefully promises to look after the respondent's financial needs."

The rational approach to the study of the quality of life is still in its infancy. In other words, we do not really have "theories" about the quality of life. But the more basic inductive approach has provided some interesting clues. The critical incidents on which it focuses are what people remember and respond to, to a greater extent than to constant factors, conditions, or states. A salary increase is more memorable than being wealthy. Often a critical incident is important because it marks the beginning of a lasting new condition: The salary increase may be remembered as the starting point of a blissful state of opulence. Thus the critical-incidents method focuses attention on concrete clues from which one can infer, at a later stage of the process of definition, the broad influences, both personal and environmental, that affect that intangible thing called the quality of life.

One of the most ambitious studies on the quality of life relying on the notion of the critical incident was reported by John Flanagan (1978) and done under the auspices of the American Institutes for Research. Three thousand Americans were asked to report incidents that had influenced their lives in a pleasant or unpleasant way. The 6,500 critical incidents so reported constituted the data on which the investigators based an initial definition of what a high or low quality of life is. These incidents fit into the following categories: material and physical well-being; social relationships; social, community, and civic activities; personal development and fulfillment; and recreation.

Flanagan's categories tell us much about the quality of life by pointing to the things on which it depends. More specifically, they allow us to ponder the relationship between work performance and the quality of life. To what extent, for example, does work of different kinds contribute to the worker's quality of life by facilitating personal development and fulfillment?

A Holistic Approach: The Systems View of the Quality of Life

The analytical exploration of the various aspects of the quality of life reveals that it is more than the sum of its parts, that ultimately a holistic stance must also be assumed if it is to be understood. Flanagan's research provides, for example, a list of conditions that are likely to cause people to report a high quality of life. But which of these conditions are primarily aspects or functions of the person? Which ones are primarily attributable to the environment? How do personal and environmental factors interact among and with each other to produce a high or low quality of life?

We are part of a social system. The quality of life is likely to be high when this system is reasonably stable, when it is not in the process of collapse. Two factors contribute, according to Fred Knelman (1981), to the possibility of a crash. First, the subsystems of our system, our society, have become isolated from each other. Bell (1976) speaks of the gap among the culture, the techno-economic structure, and the polity. Knelman points out that the relationship between politics and technology has become weaker. Technology has become autonomous, a law unto itself. It is the tail that wags the dog; the BASIC manual is more important than Plato's *Republic*. Knelman also argues that the feedback loops of our system reverberate and amplify the messages "progress is vital" and "growth is good." There are positive feedback loops here such that an increase in output feeds back a signal initiating further and destabilizing increase in output. More leads to more in a vicious circle.

To make the meaning of quality of life more explicit, we also have to look at what "quality" means in general. It appears to imply a combination of attributes or conditions that is "good" in some way. For example, the thorough, motivated, and skillful craftsman is likely to produce high quality work. The quality of the craftsman's way of working is the result of a set of attributes. These are all likely to be of value, to be desirable. But they do not *have* to be of value. Sometimes less-intelligent people do better work than more-intelligent ones, perhaps because they have to take greater care to learn things. Sometimes less-motivated people do better work than more-motivated ones, perhaps because they are less tense and anxious. What is important is that the *combination* of attributes be a propitious one. Quality is thus more than the sum of usually desirable characteristics. It is a whole, a *gestalt*, an emergent.

These statements about quality do not define it. They simply suggest what it might be. But while it is difficult to define quality, examples of it can be pointed to with reasonable confidence that others will agree that they are indeed examples of quality. In other words, while verbal, rational, or conceptual definition may be difficult, ostensive definition by pointing to examples is once again possible and the likely first step.

We can speak of the quality of life offered by a system; for example, the United States offers a high quality of life which attracts legal and illegal immigrants by the hundreds of thousands each year. We can also look at the quality of life on the micro level of an individual in a certain environment. If we want to define the term *quality of life* ostensively, we can point to different persons in different states of mind that reflect the degree to which there is a balance between them and their environments. For example, the quality of life of one particular person may be high because he has finally been able to retire and devote himself to his stamp collection; that of another may be low because she is unable to find a job that allows her to feel that she is pulling her own weight independently of husband or welfare agencies.

Sometimes the degree of balance attained between the person and the environment is primarily a function of the person; sometimes it is primarily a function of the environment. In this environment-oriented age we often think that a balance is bound to exist when the physical, economic, and social environments generously supply the clean air, the nutritious food, and the esteem and status we no doubt richly deserve. But the quality of life can be high in an unfriendly environment, provided the person comes to terms with it. Some undemanding Mexican farmers are as contented eating their corn as some rich Texans on the other side of the Rio Grande eating their steaks.

THE QUALITY OF WORKING LIFE (QWL)

Since the typical adult spends close to 40 hours per week on the job, an important aspect of the quality of life is the quality of working life. In the context of the quality of life, life is broadly defined to include work; that is, the quality of working life is traditionally treated as an aspect of the quality of life.

The quality of working life refers to the degree to which a person's work offers opportunities to experience satisfaction. The objective of job design is often, as we have seen, to raise the quality of working life by enlarging or enriching jobs, or by changing their contexts so the workers are involved in the decisions that affect what they do.

Often a high level of work satisfaction is a visible index of a high quality of working life. If that is correct, the QWL does not seem to be very high for most workers today. It is sometimes said that work satisfaction is low, that workers suffer from low morale, that they do not care about their work or that they care less about it than 30 years ago. However, the evidence on the level of work satisfaction is often conflicting, and sometimes the same evidence is interpreted differently by authors of different ideological persuasions.

One way to clarify the issue is to distinguish between the different types of evidence available. Surveys have yielded conflicting results, partly because conditions change and partly because results depend on the nature of the questions asked. Some surveys use broad and structured items ("Are you happy with your work?"—*Yes* or *No*). Given such global questions, the vast majority of workers indicate, and have always indicated, that they are "satisfied." This indication of general satisfaction may reflect a desire to avoid cognitive dissonance: To admit that one's work is boring and unsatisfactory is often the same as admitting that one is a failure (e.g., Tausky, 1978, 95).

Other surveys ask specific questions ("Would you choose the same work again?" See Tausky, 1978, 97; O'Toole, 1973, 13-17). There are also questions asked as part of intensive interviews of the type conducted by Studs Terkel (1972) for his book *Working*. O'Toole suggests that when interviewed individually, workers proved to be "full of bitterness about the conditions under which they toiled, and full of expletives that conveyed their frustration" (1974, 6).

Reviewing objective evidence such as absenteeism rates and job turnover ("quit rates") in the early 1970s, Berg (1974) noted that while there was much concern on the part of managers and others about "withdrawal of efficiency" and "strategies of independence," the evidence indicated that people would rather work than be on welfare. He also noted that "evidence that workers are misbehaving as never before is less than abundant" (p. 35). Gooding (1972), on the other hand, maintained that there was a work motivation crisis of severe proportions.

In general, the routinization and standardization of work and the deskilling of workers have probably not done much for work satisfaction. But work satisfaction has been low since the beginning of the industrial age. Few have expressed the discontent of the worker more eloquently than Karl Marx and Friedrich Engels.

Defining Work Satisfaction

Work satisfaction, or job satisfaction, has been defined as a set of attitudes held by workers toward their work. Attitudes are predispositions to evaluate things as good or bad. They can be broad or specific; they may be salient or peripheral to a person; they may be associated with action or may be strictly cognitive.

In a somewhat more expansive manner, work satisfaction has been defined by Landy and Trumbo (1976) as the "feeling which develops when you approach or anticipate approaching the job . . . the feeling in your stomach, shoulders, forehead, and chest" (p. 361). They point out that if "your drive to work is habitually accompanied by a tight uncomfortable stomach, the beginnings of a headache, tense muscles, and breathing that is not as relaxed as it should be, you can be safely described as 'dissatisfied' with your job" (p. 361).

These are working definitions. As we saw in the context of performance, the next level of definition is that of operational definitions. As McCormick and Ilgen (1985, 317) point out, work satisfaction can be measured by standardized scales and by tailor-made scales. The former fit a wide range of situations reasonably well; the latter fit a particular case with greater precision. Tailor-made scales typically assume one of the basic two forms of attitude scales: Thurstone's previously weighted statements (Thurstone and Chave, 1929) and Likert's currently rated statements (Likert, 1932). Standardized measures include the Job Descriptive Index (Smith, Kendall, and Hulin, 1969) and the Minnesota Satisfaction Questionnaire (Weiss et al., 1967).

This hurried survey brings us to conceptual (i.e., theory-based) definitions. These rely heavily on theories of work motivation because such theories typically cover both work motivation and work satisfaction. McCormick and Ilgen point out that while work motivation deals with behavior and work satisfaction deals with feelings, it is usually assumed that "individuals are motivated to seek that which is pleasant to them" (1980, 306). Work satisfaction and work motivation thus overlap, and theories of work motivation like that of Vroom (1964) underlie our attempts to approach work satisfaction on a more conceptual level.

On this level, work satisfaction is related to the perceived attractiveness (desirability, valence) of "standard performance" (Graen, 1969). Terence Mitchell and Anthony Biglan (1971) call Vroom's first postulate his "job satisfaction" model: The greater the positive valences and the greater the probability of attaining them, the greater job satisfaction will be. George Graen's definition follows from his extension of Vroom's theory. Work satisfaction has also been defined on the conceptual level as the degree to which the perceived amount that should be received is similar to the perceived amount actually received. This is the definition of Lawler (1973), obtained by combining discrepancy and equity theory, that is, the theories of Locke (1969) and of J. Stacy Adams (1965).

Work satisfaction can also be defined in part by distinguishing it from the quality of life and from work motivation. Just as the quality of working life is one aspect of the broader entity called quality of life, so it is only one of several determinants of work satisfaction. It refers to the degree to which external conditions of the work environment permit work satisfaction. The latter is determined not only by the environment, however, but also by the worker or person. The modern "new breed" workers (Yankelovich, 1979, 1981), for example, have higher expectations than their grandparents. As a result, even materially improved working conditions (higher wages, union and worker rights, and so forth) have not necessarily increased work satisfaction.

The key to differentiating work satisfaction and work motivation is the notion of contingency. Work satisfaction is easily confused with work motivation. There is a popular belief that workers who are satisfied with their jobs and bosses will show up on the job whistling a merry tune, ready to pull up their sleeves and to work hard. A little reflection suffices, however, to reveal that this is not necessarily the case. A worker may be satisfied with a job precisely because it does not require effort and affords ample opportunity for closing the office door for a quick snort or snooze. Only if work satisfaction is contingent on performance does it reinforce it and generate work motivation.

Work Satisfaction as Determinant and Consequence of Work Performance

The objective of this chapter is to show that the real bottom line of work performance is the quality of life, both because effects on the quality of life are the ultimate consequences of any human effort and because the quality of life is often an indirect determinant of future work performance. In other words, the quality of life can be both cause and effect of work performance. This can best be illustrated by means of work satisfaction, the most obvious indicator of the quality of working life.

When workers stay home, change jobs, or have accidents due to carelessness, performance is likely to be low. Regardless of whether workers are motivated and able to do the job or not, they must be *on* the job in order to perform. This raises the question of whether work satisfaction, pertaining to feelings, affects work behavior. Are satisfied workers less likely to be absent, less likely to engage in sabotage and strikes, less likely to spend their time filing grievances and looking for other jobs, less likely to have accidents? If such relationships can be demonstrated, work satisfaction can be regarded as an indirect determinant of work performance.

McCormick and Ilgen (1985) summarize the evidence by suggesting that when work satisfaction is high, job turnover will usually be low, that high work satisfaction will lead to low absenteeism rates unless other factors intervene, and that even the multidetermined entity called performance may be related, albeit in complex ways, to work satisfaction.

This suggests that work satisfaction can be an indirect and perhaps even a direct determinant of work performance. Is the reverse also true? Does work performance affect work motivation? Work satisfaction certainly appears to be among the consequences of work performance under two quite different sets of circumstances.

First, performance may be intrinsically satisfying if the job is challenging and if the worker has achievement needs, wants to grow and develop, and finds the successful accomplishment of challenging work tasks rewarding. Under these conditions, work satisfaction is intrinsically contingent on performance; this type of satisfaction can be obtained only by doing a good job.

Second, performance can be satisfying (or, at least, it can reduce dissatisfaction) when the work situation is arranged so that performance leads to extrinsic rewards. Pay, praise, promotions, and so forth are usually arranged to be contingent on high performance. We have seen that such arrangements are more typical of the free-enterprise economies than of the socialist ones.

These effects of high work performance are among the effects on the quality of life that are the topic of the next chapter. What is important to note here is that work satisfaction and work performance form a feedback loop which provides a framework within which one can more closely examine the relationship between work satisfaction—and the quality of working life and the quality of life it reflects—and work performance.

Whether work satisfaction appears in the guise of cause or effect depends on the point at which one enters the loop. Performance can generate satisfaction. Exactly how that satisfaction affects performance in turn is a matter on which behaviorists and cognitive psychologists disagree. The former presumably see it as a reinforcer contingent on, and hence strengthening, stimulus-response connections underlying performance in a particular context. The latter are likely to see it as a goal to be attained by means of high performance. Both would agree, however, that satisfaction in turn can affect work performance.

12.

Effects of Performance on the Quality of Life

Two points made earlier are particularly important from the point of view of this chapter. The first is that the ultimate goal, the real bottom line, is not performance, success, productivity, or wealth, but a high quality of life. The second is that work performance is an important means, from the point of view both of the individual and of society, to attain this ultimate goal. The preceding chapter has described the goal to be achieved; we now need to know how performance can help us achieve it by its various effects on the worker, the work environment, and the broader environment provided by society-at-large.

This brings us back, full circle, to Exhibit 1-1 in Chapter 1. Work is the activity within the work situation; it is the throughput of the worker-work environment system. This throughput includes effects on both the worker and the work environment, that is, on both subsystems of the work situation. The output of the work situation as a whole, the result of work, affects the general environment, here considered to consist of physical, economic, and social subsystems.

EFFECTS ON THE WORKER

The previous chapter concluded that high work performance is likely to increase work satisfaction, either because it meets intrinsic needs for challenge and achievement or because extrinsic rewards have been made contingent on high performance by the employer or by society. It also concluded that an increase in work satisfaction has the potential of increasing work motivation.

The effects of work performance on the second main category of relevant worker characteristics, those pertaining to ability, have also been alluded to earlier. A high level of performance fosters personality development: New knowledge and abilities are acquired in the process of doing one's work well if the job is designed to offer a reasonable degree of challenge. In certain circumstances even routine work can be challenging and growth-promoting (e.g., Misumi, 1982).

These effects on motivation and on ability are related. The reason high performance may be satisfying to the person with a high need to be effective may very well be the fact that the work is challenging and offers the opportunity to acquire new abilities that will enable the worker to operate at ever-higher levels of effectiveness in the future.

Relationships Between Work Satisfaction and Life Satisfaction

The question that now arises is whether work satisfaction, which clearly is a result of work performance in many circumstances, can carry over into life beyond the workplace. Is work satisfaction a determinant of life satisfaction? If it is, then work performance generates not only work satisfaction but also life satisfaction. Since life satisfaction is probably even more central to a person's quality of life than work satisfaction, such a relationship would mean that work performance has very direct implications for the quality of life.

Theoretically there are many different possible relationships that could exist between work satisfaction and life satisfaction. The most important of these has just been mentioned. In order to understand it better, it is useful to look at it in the context of the other possibilities.

The identity hypothesis. Perhaps work satisfaction and life satisfaction are essentially the same thing; perhaps they are so closely related and affect each other in such reciprocal and complex ways that it is impossible to distinguish them. In other words, people may integrate their work and their life to such a degree that satisfaction cannot be clearly linked to either work or nonwork (Mansfield, 1972).

The segmentation hypothesis. The second possibility is the exact opposite of the first. Work satisfaction and life satisfaction may be unrelated to each other. The chief proponent of this position is Robert Dubin (1958, 1973; see also London, Crandall, and Seals, 1977).

Effects of life satisfaction on work satisfaction. Next is the possibility that life satisfaction affects work satisfaction, that the happy *pater familias* or the fulfilled mother is also a happy worker. A relationship of this nature underlies the analyses of Weber (1958) and Arne Kalleberg (1977). Both postulate that the values of workers, transmitted to them by the culture in which they are raised, determine attitudes toward the job—attitudes that may take the form of the famous work ethic.

Theoretically, it is also possible that the two are negatively rather than positively related, that high life satisfaction somehow lowers work satisfaction or that low life satisfaction somehow raises work satisfaction. This is the possibility that seems most compatible with Bell's dichotomy between the culture and the techno-economic structure. The culture raises expectations and preaches values incompatible with the needs of the workplace. In this case, high life satisfaction made possible by a permissive culture that is growth- and individual-oriented would be associated with particularly low work satisfaction attributable to the still-industrial values of the techno-economic structure that clash dramatically with the postindistrial values of the culture. On the other hand, a low life satisfaction–high work satisfaction pattern may exist, at least on the surface, in the case of some workaholics who escape the problems of the home by rushing off to the pristine and orderly world of their offices.

Effects of work satisfaction on life satisfaction. This brings us to the possibility of direct interest to the argument that work performance has important implications for the quality of life. There is some evidence to support the hypothesis that work satisfaction (assumed to result from work performance) affects life satisfaction. Christopher Orpen concludes from a study using a cross-lagged correlation design, involving measures of work and nonwork satisfaction taken at two different times, that "the direction of causality from work to nonwork satisfaction is stronger than that in the opposite direction" (1978, 530).

Nature of the Effects of Work Satisfaction on Life Satisfaction

If work satisfaction affects life satisfaction, it can logically do so in one or more of four ways. These four contingencies are shown in Exhibit 12-1.

Low work satisfaction as cause of low life satisfaction. When the job is seen as something undesirable and frustrating, the worker may go home and bury himself behind a six-pack and watch football on TV. This is *passive generalization* (Kabanoff, 1980) of the type manifested by Arthur Kornhauser's (1965) and Harold Wilensky's (1960) workers who after a mind-numbing day on the assembly line fail to experience great joy at home.

Low work satisfaction as cause of high life satisfaction. Thomas Kando and Worth Summers (1971) have distinguished between supplemental and reactive compensation. Supplemental compensation manifests itself in the search for satisfactions off the job that the job cannot provide. It may manifest itself in the passionate pursuit of hobbies like stamp collecting on the part of the worker who operates a forklift truck in a warehouse in which there are no aesthetic satisfactions. Again, the relationship between work satisfaction and life satisfaction would be a negative one: Low work satisfaction is associated with high life satisfaction.

Reactive compensation involves a job that not merely fails to provide desirable experiences, but that is characterized by downright unpleasant

Exhibit 12-1
Postulated Effects of Work Satisfaction on Life Satisfaction

Work satisfaction (cause)	Life satisfaction (effect)	
	low	high
Low	Generalization hypothesis (Wilensky), specifically: passive generalization (Kabanoff)	Compensatory hypothesis (Wilensky), specifically: supplemental compensation (Kando & Summers)
High		Generalization hypothesis (Wilensky), specifically: active generalization (Kabanoff)

ones. These are compensated for in the personal sphere by letting off steam. This behavior pattern is characteristic of the workers described by Marx (1975) who are alienated from the product they help make, from the fragmented production process in which they play a minuscule role, and from their own selves. The relationship between work satisfaction and life satisfaction need be neither positive nor negative, although the off-the-job behavior is clearly compensatory to that on the job. The harsh discipline imposed in the factories of the Industrial Revolution in Britain and in the auto plants in the United States has generated frustration and violence. Rigid ritual on the job made way for uninhibited expression of rage.

High work satisfaction as cause of low life satisfaction. High work satisfaction could conceivably also lead to lowered life satisfaction. Perhaps some workers enjoy their work so much that their personal life appears to be, by contrast, a somewhat boring letdown. While this contingency is rationally possible, there does not appear to be much empirical evidence to suggest that it is common.

High work satisfaction as cause of high life satisfaction. When the job is seen as desirable, the positive attitude it elicits may generalize to the home. This would be active generalization (Kabanoff, 1980), illustrated by the challenged and creative systems analyst who goes home to play chess on a personal computer. It is this possibility of active generalization that highlights the importance of job satisfaction and its link to the more general notion of the quality of life.

Exhibit 12-1 and the preceding discussion reflect two quite different views on the relationship between work satisfaction and life satisfaction. These views, stated by Wilensky (1960), apply to the relationship regardless of whether it is assumed that work satisfaction is cause and life satisfaction is effect or vice versa. The first is the generalization hypothesis which states that satisfaction or dissatisfaction in one sphere carries over to the other. The second is the compensatory hypothesis according to which compensatory efforts are made to obtain satisfaction in one sphere, if such satisfaction is not available in the other. This suggests that the weakest cell in Exhibit 12-1 is the high work satisfaction-low life satisfaction cell. Given the assumption that work satisfaction is the cause and life satisfaction the effect, it fits neither a generalization nor a compensatory model.

Fusing Work Satisfaction and Life Satisfaction: Craftsmanship

C. Wright Mills writes that craftsmen combine "the simple self-expression of play and the creation of ulterior value of work . . . in work-as-craftsmanship," that they are "at work and at play in the same act," and that they "understand the meaning of [their] exertion" (1951, 221-222). Pirsig is impressed by the fact that "the material and [their] thoughts are changing together in a progression of changes until [their minds are] at rest at the same time the material's right" (1975, 161).

For some, craftsmanship is still, or has become, a way of life that teaches us much about the effect of work at its best on the worker. One exponent of this minority is Carla Needleman (1979), author of *The Work of Craft*. In her introspective analysis, craftsmanship emerges as the indigenous Western equivalent of Buddhist meditation. As "a potter" and "as a person," she tries to go beyond the "desire to succeed" (pp. 5-6), and she tries to put her analytical, restlessly categorizing, and simplifying mind in its place so that it cannot destroy the experience of crafting by labeling its diverse facets and storing them in the appropriate memory files. To her, pottery is the "struggle with the clay and with myself" (p. 42) from which grows "the craft of being human" (p. 12) whose material is not clay, but the much tougher substance of oneself.

Pottery is Needleman's means to patience, peace of mind, and the ability to refrain from judging. It teaches her to be content with less than perfection, with the product that expresses her (flawed) self. "It's a decent pot with some not too obvious flaws" (p. 5), she decides in one case, expressing a certain contentment rather than competitive perfectionism. "The object looks like me," she notes, "not physically but actually" (p. 51). Her craft opens the possibility of leaving the ego and the personal behind and of becoming an individual that is both a "dependent part of a greater whole" (p. 46) and something unique that functions independently. It allows her to "rediscover the connectedness between the inner and the outer through working directly on a material with the body and the best of [her] understanding" (p. 48).

Needleman approaches her craft in the spirit of the "little way" of St. Theresa of Lisieux, whom Lawrence LeShan described as "doing all the small tasks of everyday life [as if each] was the most important thing to be doing at that moment" (1975, 37). One is reminded of the Buddhist monk sweeping the temple and boiling the rice, and perhaps of the Honda worker of Sayama City checking the welds of the cars rolling off the assembly line.

EFFECTS ON THE WORK ENVIRONMENT

This section of the chapter is very short, but it deals with a class of effects of work performance distinct from those in the other sections, and it cannot be incorporated into them. Its objective is merely to illustrate effects on the performer's work environment. The focus is on the immediate work environment and the effects illustrated are direct and indirect.

Suppose a worker's performance manifests itself in the discovery of new ways of doing the work more effectively. The new ways may be adopted informally by co-workers; his contribution may be recognized by the supervisor; management may adopt the new procedures formally. In the process, the attitude of all of these agents of the work environment changes; the nature of the work itself changes as new tasks are defined and old ones deleted. Performance here has direct effects on the work environment. Whether the effect is a major one, assuming the form of new company policy, depends in large part on the worker's job. Major changes are more likely if the performer is a manager and less likely if a front-line worker. However, modern job design efforts rely heavily on input from the people on the front actually doing the work under review.

Performance may also change the work environment of the performer indirectly. The performer may be assigned new responsibilities, may be given a more spacious office, may be invited to staff conferences (Burke, 1982). The work organization remains unchanged; the work environment is not changed in an absolute way. It only changes relative to the performer who climbs the career ladder and is exposed to a different part of it.

Of course, performance does not invariably lead to promotion. After all, there may be a "flight from merit" and some organizations, especially large ones like the civil services, may find it less difficult to promote on the basis of seniority than on the basis of performance. On the other hand, such flights from merit may not be profitable. Astute managers are thus likely to persist in old-fashioned ways and to move performers demonstrating merit into positions of increased responsibility and greater challenge. At least in some organizations the worker can thus change the work environment and possibly raise the quality of working life by being a performer.

EFFECTS ON THE BROADER ENVIRONMENT

Science fiction offers some chilling depictions of low-quality broader environments. In *The Dosadi Experiment,* Frank Herbert (1978) depicts *Chu,* a city of 19 million inhabitants who live in huge towers if they have status and power and who scavenge in endless "warrens" if they don't. Food has to be processed in factories to remove the poison that permeates everything on the planet outside the city. The inhabitants ravenously devour slop as if it were caviar, grateful that it will not kill them. The inhabitants of *Chu* live in an urban hell, but what lies beyond the rim around them is even worse: a poisoned environment of desert and rock populated by Rim Rabble desperately trying to infiltrate the city whose depoisoned garbage they covet as if it were nectar and ambrosia.

Another uninspiring environment is described by Walter Miller (1959) in *A Canticle for Leibowitz.* The scene is set 500 years after a nuclear holocaust that separated a gentleman named Leibowitz from a slip of paper reminding him to get a pound of pastrami. The slip survived, a treasured archeological find of the postdeluge or postholocaust era. Not that this new age is one of flourishing science. The earth is populated with grotesque humanoid mutations, and there are a few genetically unscathed farmers and monks trying to survive in primitive villages and isolated monasteries.

The quality of our broader environment is an important aspect of the quality of life. Reginald Holme and Gordon Perry (1977), for example, discuss the quality of life primarily as something that depends on the manmade environment (brute-force large-scale development, concrete expanse architecture), the natural environment (overexploited and polluted), methods of production (mass production rather than craftsmanship), ways of spending leisure constructively, and community life (arm's-length relationships with fellow citizens). While one must guard against blind environment orientedness, the quality of life does presuppose a number of conditions that must prevail in the physical, economic, and social environments.

These conditions become matters of interest and concern in a sequential fashion parallel to Maslow's hierarchy of needs. First, physical conditions that permit life in the first place must prevail. Second, the standard of living must be sufficiently high to permit doing things other than grazing goats and sowing wheat. There must be at least occasional freedom from the necessity to struggle for survival, a certain amount of wealth that is distributed fairly. At this level the conditions of interest are economic. Finally, social conditions that make life secure and that allow growth and development must prevail. Such conditions should make it possible for people to develop ways of spending their free time constructively.

The quality of life is thus said to be high when the air is clean, the water is uncontaminated, and the land is neither oozing with toxic wastes nor obscured by crassly commercial billboards nor covered with concrete. It is said to be high when goods and services are available and of high quality. Finally, it is said to be high when the social fabric is strong, when the cab driver is helpful, and when bystanders can be counted on to do more than gawk or pretend they are blind.

This final section explores some ways in which the quality of the physical, economic, and social environments depends on work performance, on the quality of the work done. With respect to each of these environments the following questions can be raised:

1. What does it include? Do the physical, economic, and social environments constitute meaningful entities that can be analyzed separately, for which particular effects of high performance can be identified?
2. Are efforts to improve the quality of the particular environment useful, important, or even essential?
3. Do steps to raise performance levels constitute a promising possibility for raising the quality of the particular environment?

The Physical Environment

In the passages just quoted, both Herbert and Miller point to threats to the quality of the physical environment, that is, the quality of life that the physical environment can make possible. There are more human beings than this planet can support in the manner to which many of them have become accustomed. The age of bulldozer technology may be over. Natural resources have to be rationed and used in the most efficient way possible. In the past, capital-intensive technology was the preferred mode of processing natural resources. The costs in pollution and energy of such technology now turn out to be more than we can afford.

The subject of work performance assumes a particular significance in the context of the threatened physical environment. The alternative to a systems crash may be greater reliance on human resources and the sophisticated information-processing technology these resources can provide.

This means restraint in the use of huge bulldozers to dig little holes for planting trees—bulldozers that not only devour fuel and pollute the air, but that damage the landscape in a way that creates more work to be corrected by the gentler interventions of human labor than digging the holes by hand would have in the first place. It does place a premium on competence, on competent individuals who "work smarter" and who can make the most of the least.

The road ahead, if we wish to avoid the narrow, overcrowded, and oppressive warrens of Dosadi, is suggested by the title of a book by British author Brian Rothery (1972), *Survival by Competence*. Rothery notes that "systems of unlimited resources tolerate incompetence and waste, but systems of limited resources cannot tolerate either" (p. 1).

One would think that nuclear technology calls for the highest standards of performance on the part of all those involved in deploying it, maintaining it, and managing it. After all, they are not merely playing with dynamite. Yet nuclear technology is handled with amazing nonchalance.

The Three Mile Island incident is only one of many incidents that give sleepless nights to many citizens.

John Fuller cites a document which declares that "the workmanship going into nuclear power plant construction is far from adequate. The increasing number of quality assurance problems, maintenance deficiencies, management review oversights, and operator errors is disturbing" (1975, p. 121). Fuller describes one worker's perception of a construction site: "No one quite seemed to know what he was doing. It wasn't like the old days . . . when the welding was clean and tight" (p. 225). Fuller also cites an Atomic Energy Commission study reporting 850 "abnormal occurrences" such as "design and manufacturing errors, . . . operator mistakes, faulty maintenance, . . . and bad quality control" (p. 229). The point here is not so much that standards of workmanship and operation are low; they are no doubt higher than in many other settings. The point is that in this industry they must be, but are not, incredibly high.

One of the things that "spaceship earth," with its diminishing natural resources and its increasing reliance on nuclear energy, needs is many, many individuals whose work performance is very, very high.

The Economic Environment

In the Middle Ages the popular imagination produced a mythical country dramatically different from the worlds of Frank Herbert and Walter Miller. Its lakes are filled with milk and honey; houses are made of cake; rivers of wine flow through groves of fruit-laden trees; roasted pheasants fly around practically begging to be eaten; buttered larks fall from the sky into the open mouths of snoring gourmets. In Italy they called this country *il paese di Cuccagna*. In Germany they called it *Schlaraffenland*. In England it was known as the *land of Cockaigne*.

What the imagination of the toiling and usually deprived populace of the Middle Ages produced is a vision of a society that does not require work and in which everything one could possibly desire is immediately available. In this vision, work appears as something devoutly to be avoided and material goods are seen as things devoutly to be desired. The concerns about work and about goods reflected by this "cake-land" fantasy are economic ones.

The word *economy* is derived from the Greek words *oikos* (house) and *nemein* (to distribute). But whether it is on the level of the individual household or that of a complex society, economics is concerned with how human needs for material things are met in a systematic and reasonably premeditated way. When we look at the economic factors affecting the quality of life, we are thus going beyond the physical environment that makes life possible to the economic environment that can create a cushion between necessity and what one would like to do.

The Availability and Quality of Products

The progress of the United States toward a state of abundance has been rapid and the envy of a fascinated world. American enterprise, engineering, innovation, and management techniques have generated a flood of goods that almost threatens to sweep unwary consumers off their feet. Only recently have economic turbulences allowed other countries to overtake the United States in the standard-of-living sweepstakes. Americans still eat more beef and burn more oil per capita than any other nation. Roasted pheasants do not actually fly through the air, but thanks to Colonel Sanders, abundant supplies of fried chicken are available at almost every street corner. The supermarkets and department stores offer inexhaustible supplies that challenge even the clouds of ravenous locusts that descend on them on Fridays and Saturdays.

American technology is certainly able to deliver the goods. In general, the quality of goods is high. There are, however, exceptions. The quality of life is certainly not enhanced by houses that begin to sag a few weeks after the buyer has moved in, by new cars that fall apart on the drive home from the showroom, by computers that do not come to life when they have been unwrapped, or by appliances that exhibit a temper and will of their own.

The human component is an important part of the productive system that generates products of inadequate quality. The supervisor cannot worry about an ulcer instead of the rattles in the cars that are passing by on the conveyor belt. The worker cannot drop a screw into the disk drive case and reach for another one instead of retrieving and using the first. The manager cannot order cheaper leather for the shoe factory on the assumption that it will last a little longer than the warranty on the shoes. On all levels, decisions are made daily that are either wise and authentic or that lead to low-quality products and questionable contributions to the quality of life.

Competent and Incompetent Service

Bell (1973) equates postindustrial society and service society. Before this bold assertion conjures up visions of nuns staffing the schools for a pittance, boy scouts helping overburdened housewives with the grocery bags, and doctors rushing to make housecalls in the middle of the night, it should be added that service society in this context simply means that a majority of the workforce is engaged in the service sector of the economy rather than in manufacturing or agriculture. Bell's assertion implies nothing about the quality of services rendered. But in the society in which the service sector dominates, the quality of life depends to a great extent on the quality of service, that is, on whether the multitudes employed in the service sector provide real service or whether they grimly occupy service jobs and go through the motions.

Economics is concerned with the creation and distribution of wealth, and wealth includes both goods and services because they have utility (i.e., satisfy human needs and hence find ready buyers). From the point of view of this chapter, goods and services differ, however, in one important way. Unlike economic goods, services have often more than purely economic significance. This section concerns economic services. That means services that typically are rendered in the private sector for a price. Here, too, improvement is possible. The sluggish waiter or waitress, the uninformed sales clerk, the nurse impatient to get back to the ward office and a cup of coffee, the careless and bumbling repairman, the doctor who is in a hurry—none of these contribute to the quality of life of the people they service rather than serve.

In the provision of services, the human component is even more important than it is in industrial production. Book sellers who value books, who read widely, who understand the mechanics of dealing with publishers, and who have built contacts in the business; secretaries who can fill in the blanks left in the boss's dictated letters; fast-food outlet employees who catch the greasy onion rings before they end up on the disgusted customer's tray—all of these remain important and cannot easily be replaced by technology.

The Social Environment

Work performance also affects the most elusive of our three environments: the social environment, which becomes a matter of increasing interest when the physical conditions of life exist and when the economic environment permits the luxury of looking beyond the next few meals, cold spells, mortgage payments, and frayed suits.

The three samples of Flanagan's (1978) American Institutes for Research study mentioned earlier identified the following specific social factors reflecting various aspects of the culture that affected their quality of life: relationships with parents, brothers, sisters, and relatives; having and raising children; sexual relationships; relationships with close friends; community and civic activities; and recreational activities (such as sports and playing cards, giving parties, and meeting other people).

Not only did these samples identify a relatively large number of social determinants of the quality of life, they also attached great importance to them. Economic determinants affecting the level of material well-being were rated as less important, probably because in the still relatively affluent society they are not particularly pressing. Physical conditions like clean air or clean water were hardly mentioned. Although pollution is a problem from coast to coast, its effects are really only noticed when it is too late.

In the social environment too there is considerable room for raising the quality of life through higher levels of work performance. At its best, a community reinforces the web of social relationships that provide support and a sense of security. In practice, however, modern American communities are neither supportive nor secure. The suburbs sprawl uniformly over many square miles and promote anonymity rather than active participation in grass-roots politics. The inner-city ghettoes are tense; muggers roam their streets, and many law-abiding citizens try to get back to the relative security of their homes before sunset. Everywhere trash piles up, burning cigarette butts fly out the windows of speeding cars, motorcycle engines are revved up in the middle of the night, stereo sets blare away in the neighbor's apartment and in passing cars. Those who seek to escape find that wails of the superstars of rock and punk are carried by transistorized weekend hikers into the remotest corners of the American wilderness. There is carelessness, lack of civility, aggression that quickly flares into mayhem, and the apathy summed up in the famous phrase: "I don't want to get involved."

Higher work performance will certainly not cure all of these ills. But it could reduce them. Policemen, city officials, social workers, our favorite cab drivers, and many others could have a marked impact on the quality of our social environments by doing their jobs well. Effective teachers might have an influence that could lead to fewer boom boxes shattering the quiet of the night and more evidence of consideration and civility. Ultimately the problem goes much further and one must rely on higher levels of performance, not just in the role of worker but also in the role of parent and citizen. Our roles as workers often merge imperceptibly into these other roles.

Our lives are doubtless of higher quality when the teachers care, when the policemen respect our civil rights, when the bureaucrats don't just pass the buck, when the lawyers seek justice rather than loopholes. In other words, life is of higher quality when work performance is of high quality, when the cab driver is willing to step out of his car to assist the elderly passenger even if no job description says he must do so and even if no supervisor is watching.

People on every stratum and in every niche of the techno-economic structure who do their work competently can thus improve the quality of the physical, economic, and social environments. They also improve the quality of their own personal state by generating satisfaction of both basic and higher level needs, and they contribute to the quality of their work environment.

Work performance of high quality thus contributes to many aspects of the quality of life. It does so without using additional natural resources; in fact, it may lead to their more efficient use. Somehow competent work performance looks suspiciously like the golden road to a higher quality of life in a future of possible scarcity.

13.

Implications for the Search for Excellence

The question that has been raised before in the context of motivation and ability rises again, now that the whole tool kit of basic concepts has been laid out. How can these tools be used to attain the higher quality of life, for the people doing the work themselves as well as for the beneficiaries of their work, which results from better work performance?

There are no simple answers, no quick fixes, no esoteric regimens guaranteed to turn around a moribund organization or boost a sagging career. However, the basics assembled here can cause us to look at the immediate issues in front of us intensively and in their wider context.

More specifically, what the argument presented in this book implies for people at work striving for excellence can be summed up in five points:

1. Ultimately our objectives should go beyond quality as means for attaining success and profit to quality as an end in itself, beyond the concerns of the sphere of work to the broader concerns of the sphere of life.

2. While leaders are important, in the final analysis it is people at all levels of the work organization who do, or do not do, "good work."

3. "Good work" of the type done by the motivated and able (competent) craftsman is still an admirable model for excellent work performance.

4. Work performance at all levels is enhanced by awareness of what the scientific efforts in such areas as industrial and organizational psychology, management science, and industrial engineering can tell us about the motivation and ability of individuals and about organizing individuals, tools, and resources as effective wholes.

5. The complex and changing problems facing the person at work call for an eclectic frame of mind and a skeptical attitude toward vigorously advertised simple solutions and techniques.

QUALITY AS MEANS AND AS END

The previous two chapters focused on the notion of quality. It is an abstract and difficult concept which, fortunately, manifests itself in more concrete variants like the quality of life and the quality of working life. The chief characteristic of the quality discussed in this book is that it is generally an end in itself—a final, ultimate, and definitely "superordinate" goal. This is certainly true for the quality of life, and it usually is or ought to be true for the quality of working life.

The term *quality* is also used in another way, however. Quality as a means to greater profitability is a notion that has been rediscovered. Some organizations introduce quality-of-working-life programs in the hope of increasing productivity. The Japanese are said to produce high-quality products with which American industry cannot compete. Quality is the subject of empirical studies, using surveys and focus groups to determine what it means to the consumer. It is also one of the basics managers are told to pursue. It overlaps greatly with Tom Peters and Robert Waterman's (1982) *excellence*.

Quality as means belongs to the sphere of work, to the techno-economic structure. But we have seen that the sphere of work can and should be closely related to the sphere of life, to Daniel Bell's culture. Perhaps the sphere of life should even subsume the sphere of work so that we work to live, rather than live to work. This suggests that quality as means and quality as end need not be contradictory objectives. In fact, they usually go hand in hand because the former may not only be the means to greater profits, it can also be the means to quality as end. We have seen that products that work and last and services that are competently delivered enhance the quality of our economic environment, and that they are likely to enhance the social and even the physical environment as well.

In other words, the pursuit of quality as a means to greater and more long-term profitability is desirable if it contributes somehow to quality as end. That means the quality pursued should probably not be too esoteric or too unaffordable. If it only appeals to the peculiar or very rich, it is not doing much to raise the quality of life in general. The quality that serves as means to quality as end is more likely to be exemplified by a good nurse or a good teacher, who has a lasting positive impact on frightened patients or confused pupils.

The motivating effect on individual workers, anywhere within the organizational hierarchy, of knowing that they contribute to the quality of life and that they are doing something meaningful should not be under-estimated. We saw that goals are important in cognitive theory and on the practical level of motivating people through goal setting. Superordinate goals such as the pursuit of quality as end are somewhat different from the specific goals we encountered earlier, but they play a vital role in giving meaning to our often unpleasant duties at work, in decreasing the probability of burn-out, and in reducing alienation.

To sum up: The quality of immediate interest in work organizations is first of all a means to increased competitiveness and a more satisfactory bottom line. In addition, it should be a means to more ultimate quality such as a higher quality of life for people in general. Finally, when it is perceived as the means to attain such a more distant and "superordinate" goal, the quest for quality is likely to be a more meaningful activity than work carried out to keep the boss quiet or the shareholders happy.

LEADERS AND FIRST-LINE WORKERS

There appears to be a widespread belief that the agent of change critical to the pursuit of excellence is the chief executive officer (CEO) and that much, perhaps everything, depends on what CEOs choose to do or not to do (Peters and Austin, 1985; O'Toole, 1985). How should we interpret this trend from dispassionate management, along the lines of Weber's bureaucracy, to passionate, single-minded, visionary leadership? Is this just the pendulum swinging from one extreme to the other in its usual way, or is it the result of new insight? Is it based on more thorough understanding? Does it constitute progress?

If we follow Peters and Austin and drop the term *manager* and adopt the term *leader,* are we in some ways returning to the social structure of Toynbee's "barbarian warband," to the tough times in which the most fit led the clan, band, or tribe to assure its survival? Times are certainly a little tougher than in the first three decades after World War II, but are they *that* tough? Do we have to throw out Weber's baby, power limited by the objective and thought-out rules of a functioning bureaucracy, with the bath water of delay and inaction? Is the faith we exhibit in certain leaders by paying them million-dollar annual compensation packages justified?

The focus here has been on the individual worker; that worker may be anyone who works. The model of the situation of the individual worker presented by means of Exhibit 1-1 in Chapter 1 assumes that the worker may be anyone, from the custodian to the CEO. It is a very democratic model. It is meant to emphasize the general perspective that all those at work operate in a similar framework, are affected by similar determinants, and can have similar effects. Not only the CEO, but also the surgeon, the custodian, and the Sierra Nevada postman do work of the highest quality when they do the best that is possible under the circumstances, and especially when they do it because they want to, not because someone will give them a worker-of-the-day plaque. The focus here has been on the micro level of the individual working person. It is assumed that the macro level performance of an organization is largely a function of the joint performances of individuals.

This does not mean that the roles of leaders, managers, or CEOs and first-line workers are identical. In fact, to make the model fit the former, we have to substitute a different form of higher authority, such as the board of directors, government regulators, and the legal system for "management" and "supervisors" as extrinsic agents determining work behavior.

More important is the fact that people in key positions can have more far-reaching effects, for better or worse, than first-line workers. It is thus obviously important to look at leadership. Chapter 8 reviewed some of the basic findings on this complex subject. The social scientists distinguish between leader and position, along lines known to humanists and philosophers like Carlyle and Tolstoi long ago. When scientific research focused on leaders, it also detected with remarkable consistency two leadership styles: There are "hard" leaders who focus on production and there are "soft" leaders who focus on maintenance of the organization and its resources. The "managerial grid" of Blake and Mouton (1964) allows us to study these styles as they combine in different ways, and to begin to study how different combinations affect managerial work performance in different contexts. The scientists also point out that very different types of leaders are required in very unfavorable and favorable situations on the one hand, and in relatively neutral situations on the other. Fiedler (1971), in particular, has shown that the leaders who get along well with all of their workers do best in a neutral situation, while the tougher leaders do best when everything is working well *or* when there is a crisis.

However rudimentary the information scientists provide on this complex subject of leadership, it is more reliable information than hunches and biases. It is a beginning and it helps us ask pertinent questions. Why do some fail while others succeed? Under what conditions are different leader types or different leadership styles most effective or least effective?

The empirical scientific literature tends to focus on specifics—to contribute depth rather than scope—but these specifics are the trees that give us a more meaningful understanding of the forest of strategic decision making and the role of management. As one compares the scientific with the popular literature on management, one is struck by the fact, for example, that the modern successful leader exhibits a very sophisticated blend of the two managerial styles the scientists have identified.

It is quite a large step from the scientific evidence to answers to such broad questions as whether, or under what conditions, we are better off with leaders than with "mere" managers. But the question does pertain to the dichotomy of leader versus position, of personal power versus position power. The scientific evidence allows us at least to refine our questions, to pursue points related to them in the more technical and academic literature, and to know when we move into the realm of unsupported or barely supported opinion.

To sum up this section: While leaders are important, quality is usually not something that is principally attained through them. It is something generated and attained by the workforce as a whole, by both its leaders and the person who tightens the screws of the cars on the assembly line. Both have to ask: Did I do the best I can do? In the pursuit of quality, leadership is *one* of the important, not *the* most important, means.

"GOOD WORK"

What we mean by *quality* and *excellence* in the context of work and work organizations in the last analysis appears to be "good work." This term has been used in two ways, however. The first of these is that of the "environmental monists" in tune with the spirit of the times who mean by "quality of work" the quality of the work tasks and the work environment. From the present perspective, good work in this sense is important primarily because it makes good work in the second sense more likely.

Good work in this second sense denotes an aspect of the result of work done, a result that is at least in part a function of personal decision and effort.

We have lost track of the meaning of good work in this second sense. Even E. F. Schumacher, author of *Small Is Beautiful* (1973) and scourge of high technology and modern expertise, uses the term in the experts' sense when he writes in *Good Work:* "We should prepare [young people] to be able to distinguish between good work and bad work and encourage them not to accept the latter" (1979, 118). *Et tu, Brute!* It is true that "good work" means much more to Schumacher than to the industrial and organizational psychologist. He sees it as "work that ennobles the product as it ennobles the producer," as the path to the goal of " 'perfection,' . . . 'the kingdom,' 'salvation,' 'nirvana,' 'liberation,' 'enlightenment,' and so forth" (1979, 122). But an important thrust of his conception of good work is that it is something out there that should be, but is not, offered by the environment.

While the experts define "good work" and "quality of work" as a function of the environment and while Schumacher is somewhat ambiguous, Needleman (1979) sees it clearly as primarily the result of personal effort, as something that is reflected in the beauty and usefulness of pots, bedspreads, wooden utensils, and handknotted rugs. This way of defining quality is more closely related to the roots of the notion of quality in craftsmanship. The potter may be able to turn out 50 average cups or five high-quality ones, but since machines can produce hundreds of average ones, he is likely to opt for quality production. That does not mean that he requires the product to be perfect; it does not have to win ego-gratifying awards, but it must be something that expresses his feelings and that he does not have to disown. Craftsmen work with material and create concrete products that will have a certain permanence.

Today, of course, the "quality of work," in the sense of quality of the results of work, means no longer just graceful yet solid pots. It is more likely to mean useful contributions in providing services, made as a member of a team or as part of a large organization. We may be well advised, however, to keep the model of the craftsman alive. The women and men we lump together under this label have traits still required by the office worker in the huge cathedrals of the service industries, by the auto worker, by the professional writing a report, by the manager making personnel decisions.

SCIENCE AND GUT FEELING

Parallel to the apparent swing away from management toward rediscovered leadership, there is a swing away from science, cold logic, mathematical models, and techniques like those of decision theory, toward "gut feeling." There appears to be a feeling that the business schools have become too academic, that business professors have turned into "scholarly scribblers" (O'Toole, 1985), that the graduating MBAs are technicians unable to assume the many practical responsibilities of engaging in business and administration.

Here too one has to ask: Is the reaction too sharp? Are we going from one extreme to the other? Does the objective scientific approach not have all kinds of merit?

We saw in the preceding section that the "scholarly scribblers" can tell us a few things about leadership, and that what they can tell us forms a basis for venturing more deeply and broadly into complicated issues such as the question, "What type of leader for what type of situation?"

More generally, it is taken for granted here that there is a connection between the findings, theories, and models of the social scientists and industrial engineers on the one hand, and the behavior of workers and managers on the other, between the diverse theories of motivation and the motivated Sierra Nevada mailman, between the models of the learning process and the informed saleswoman in the department store in Zürich. We saw in the discussion of leadership immediately preceding this section that while there is a gap between the scientific understanding of leadership and what leaders do, this gap need not cause us to forget what the researchers and scientists tell us. Awareness of what the scientists can tell us has various beneficial effects anyway: It makes us aware when we speculate that we are indeed speculating rather than dealing in facts; it allows us to ask our questions at least on the basis of what is known; it provides principles and concepts of "second-order" (i.e., general) applicability. This is as true generally of the relationship between what has been established and what workers and managers need to know in their quest of quality as it is of leadership.

Working and managing without some reasonably firmly established body of knowledge is like applying behavior modification without knowing anything about learning theory or using projective tests like the Rorschach without knowing anything about perception. The trend away from the scientific basics is as marked in psychology as in business, and there are psychologist technicians interested solely in the immediately useful who are quick to move in with their aversive conditioning apparatus or their inkblots. The position taken here is that this is not the optimal way to proceed, that behavior modification is learning that can be a little better controlled and whose effects can be a little better predicted with a background in learning theory, and that responses to inkblots are the results of processes about which both the expert on perception and the one on personality can tell us a great deal. "Nothing is more useful than a good theory," as Kurt Lewin reportedly said.

While quality focuses our attention on goals, aims, or objectives and hence on its motivating effect on the work behavior of workers and managers, the primary emphasis here has generally been on the ability of workers and managers to attain quality, on the cognitive processes of attaining the knowledge of what they have to do about motivation, work-related abilities and skills, competence, and ultimately performance in their quest for quality.

Of course, understanding characterized by depth and scope is a relative thing. Some things can be understood scientifically. Others have to be approached in a humanistic and speculative frame of mind. This is the approach called for when we go beyond neatly isolated notions like "person" and "environment," or "motivation" and "ability"; when we abandon the useful fiction that things exist independently of each other and start dealing with the person-environment interaction or with competence. Still other issues call for "gut feeling." The point is that gut feeling should be relied on only when necessary and that it should be informed rather than raw and elemental.

THE ECLECTIC FRAME OF MIND

In the pursuit of quality or search for excellence we need both management and leadership, both science and gut feeling. These and other different emphases have to be balanced or synthesized. An eclectic rather than a single-minded or dogmatic frame of mind is called for. The same is true not only in the context of action, but also in the context of understanding which is the real concern of this book.

The comprehensiveness of the model of the total situation comprising the person-at-work which is depicted in Exhibit 1-1 is meant to help prevent a one-sided and unbalanced riveting of attention to whatever excites current interest, be it leadership, job enrichment, scientific management, or organizational depth psychology. The model sums up the generally eclectic approach suggested here. It lays out the factors we have to keep in mind.

This model relating the individual at work, the work situation, and the total situation is meant to function as a heuristic device that raises questions in a coherent pattern. It has done this in the development of this book summarizing findings and theories obtained and formulated by the collectivity of researchers and practitioners.

Much work remains to be done on this scientific and collective level, but the focus here is on individual workers and managers trying to apply the currently available body of knowledge relevant to their concerns. Most of us fall into this category. We have to put meat on the bones constituted by the model, so that its different components become meaningful to us and useful in our particular situations. In this manner we will come closer to developing much more specific models that suit our particular circumstances in the face of changing economic conditions, of our changing personal needs and the changing needs of the people we work with, of our different organizational settings, and of our different immediate objectives.

Appendix 1.

The Mathematical Formulations of Cattell's and Vroom's Motivation Theories

CATTELL

Cattell's extension of Lewin's basic postulate that behavior is a function of person and environment assumes the following form:

$$a_{fj} = b_{f1}s_{j1}T_1 + \ldots + b_{fk}s_{jk}T_k + \ldots + b_{fm}s_{jm}T_m.$$

a_{fj} stands for the strength of a particular course of action f in the particular situation j. This strength of the course of action manifests itself in amount and degree. For example, the strength of friendly attentiveness toward customers of Alfred M. in the shoestore would be reflected by how often and to what extent he is friendly. But Cattell is specific; he knows that Mr. M.'s attentiveness depends on the situation. Let's assume that situation j is the situation in which somebody, either the manager or the owner, is on the premises to supervise activities.

The term T_k stands for the traits or ergs of the person that enter into play in the situation j. In Mr. M.'s case, let's assume that the ergs gregariousness (T_1), self-assertion (T_2), and security (T_3) play a role. In other words, Mr. M. may be motivated by the need to interact with people, to express himself and have his way, and to feel financially secure.

The strength of the traits can be measured by administering some psychological test to Mr. M. Let's assume we do that and find that he scores high on gregariousness, low on self-assertion, and high on security. The strength of such traits is usually expressed by comparing people with other members of a sample to which they belong. For example a score of $+2$ might be a high score compared with the mean of such a sample, and -2 might be a low one. Mr. M.'s score on gregariousness might thus be a $+2$.

Instead of just looking at the global notion of personality, we are looking at three specific and empirically established personality traits. In the same way, the global notion of "environment" can also be broken down into specifics. Lewin's environment is represented here by one of the two parts of the "action indices" or weights $b_{fk}s_{jk}$ that are associated with each of the traits T_k.

The first part, b_{fk}, is the degree to which a particular trait is associated with a particular course of action. For example, gregariousness (T_1) and friendly attentiveness (a_f) may be highly correlated; b_{f1} might be 0.8. Note that coefficients of 0, $+1$, and -1 indicate no relationship, a perfect positive relationship, and a perfect negative relationship, respectively.

The second part, s_{jk}, is the degree to which the specific situation j ("supervisor present") modulates the normal expression of the trait k. For example, the presence of a supervising person might cause Mr. M. to be restrained and "professional"; he might thus subdue his gregariousness. Thus in this situation s_{j1} might be low, say 0.2. We thus have a weight for gregariousness in situation j for course of action f of $.8 \times .2 = .16$.

The following form of the more general specification equation with which we started out would fit the case of Mr. M. as described here:

$$a_{fj} = b_{f1}s_{j1}T_1 + b_{f2}s_{j2}T_2 + b_{f3}s_{j3}T_3.$$

Using the values postulated so far and other plausible values we might obtain the following result for Mr. M.'s strength of friendly attentiveness in the shoestore when the supervisor is present:

$$a_{fj} = (.8 \times .2) \times 2 + (.4 \times .2) \times (-1) + (.9 \times .8) \times 3 = 2.40.$$

Assuming that the trait scores are standard scores ranging from $+3$ to -3, the maximum strength possible is 9, so this value is not exceedingly high. Inspection of the equation and its values allows us to surmise to some extent as to why it isn't higher. Two of the modulators s_{jk} are quite low, for example, and so is a score on one of the traits positively correlated with the desired behavior. It might well be that if the supervisor were absent, more self-assertive salesmen would be friendlier, and that the owner and manager should hire more self-assertive salesmen and stay out of the store to let them do their thing. Note that in this relatively strong (i.e., specific) theory we encounter once again the multiplicative relationship discussed in Chapter 3.

VROOM

Exhibit A-1 shows Mr. M.'s situation in the form of the type of diagram commonly used by valence-instrumentality-expectancy theorists. It presents plausible effort-performance and performance-outcome expectancies, levels of effort and of performance, and second-level outcomes together with their valences that might apply to the work situation of Mr. M. in the shoestore. Six different outcomes are specified. It is assumed that each is an outcome sought for its own sake. One could argue, however, that outcomes like the paycheck are means to other ends, that they are outcomes that lead to further outcomes. An extension of the diagram could accommodate this possibility, but here the intent is to keep things simple.

The possible valences are assumed to range from -1 to $+1$; thus the highest valence of .9 associated with the outcome "satisfied owner" is indeed high, even higher than the valence of "paycheck." That is not surprising, since a satisfied employer means not only that the next paycheck will come through, but also that many more are likely to follow it. The least desirable outcome is a dissatisfied owner who might be tempted to fire the employee.

The performance-outcome expectancies in our example range from .20 to 1.00. No matter what his performance level, Mr. M. expects to receive his next paycheck. On the other hand, his expectancy that good work will produce a satisfied boss is low, perhaps because the boss seldom is in the store and gets his information indirectly from the store manager.

A look at the effort-performance expectancies indicated in the diagram shows that Mr. M. is not sure of his ability to succeed. He expects that the probability of his efforts leading to successful performance is only .40. This implies, as noted earlier, an expectancy of .60 that his efforts will produce unsuccessful performance. It will come as no surprise that he expects with certainty that no effort will lead to unsuccessful performance.

So here he is, in the store facing customers, and we are trying to predict whether he will choose to do his best or to take it easy. Fortunately, Vroom has formulated three relatively strong postulates to help answer this question. The first of his postulates is:

1. The valence $V_{k.}$ of a first-level outcome k is a function of the sum of the products of the valences V_{kj} of all relevant second-level outcomes j and the perceived probabilities (performance-outcome expectancies, instrumentalities) I_{kj} of attaining these second-level outcomes.

Let's assume that we have m different second-level outcomes and that we don't have to worry about the nature of the function relating the valence of the first-level outcomes to second-level valences and instrumentalities. Thus we have:

$$V_{k.} = V_{k1}I_{k1} + \ldots + V_{kj}I_{kj} + \ldots + V_{km}I_{km}.$$

In the case of Mr. M., given the values in Exhibit A-1 and as shown in Exhibit A-2, the valence $V_{1.}$ of successful performance is 1.68 and the valence $V_{2.}$ of unsuccessful performance is $-.08$. Thus Mr. M., not surprisingly, finds successful performance on his part more desirable than unsuccessful performance.

Exhibit A-1
Example Illustrating Valence-Instrumentality-Expectancy Theory

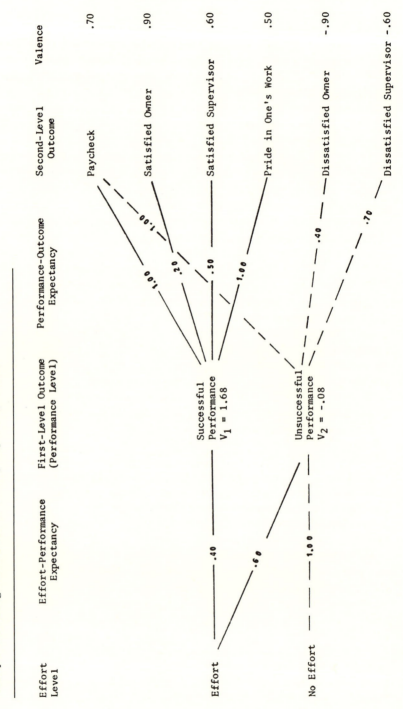

But this is not enough to allow us to predict whether he will choose to make an effort or not. For this we need to take into consideration his effort-performance expectancies. If Mr. M. believes, for example, that he is unable to provide good service no matter how hard he tries, his motivation to make the effort in what he thinks is a lost cause would probably be minimal. These effort-performance expectancies enter the picture in Vroom's second postulate:

2. The force F_p to pursue a course of action p is a function of the sum of the products of the valences V_k of all first-level outcomes k and the strengths of the person's effort-performance expectancies E_{kp} that the course of action p will lead to the attainment of these first-level outcomes.

Assuming n different primary outcomes and again ignoring the nature of the function involved, we have

$$F_p = V_1.E_{1p} + \ldots + V_k.E_{kp} + \ldots + V_n.E_{np}.$$

By means of the calculations shown in Exhibit A-2 we find that for Mr. M. the force F_1 to make an effort is .624 and the force F_2 to take it easy is $-.08$. Not only does he perceive making an effort as the more desirable alternative, he is also more inclined to actually make an effort.

Vroom's third postulate is fairly obvious and implicit in the other two, but there are advantages to expressing it explicitly:

3. A person will choose that course of action toward which he or she is pushed or pulled with the greatest force.

In the case of Mr. M., an effort will be made. It would be strange if this were not so. This explicit example makes it quite clear that the valences and hence the forces acting on an employee can be manipulated fairly easily in the typical case. One may assume that most employers know this and arrange work environments accordingly by providing appropriate positive (and perhaps negative) rewards.

This is by no means a complete analysis, but it illustrates the general approach one can take on the basis of Vroom's theory. The reader will note that both the expectancies and valences are cognitive entities—things that exist in the worker's mind. The reader will also note that the relationships between valences and expectancies are multiplicative. If either is 0, so is the product, the overall valence or the motivating force. Finally, the reader will note that there may be more than just a formal relationship between the multiplicative nature of valence and expectancy and between motivation and ability in the basic postulate *competence* = *motivation* × *ability*. Valences are certainly motivating. Furthermore, effort-performance probabilities depend on ability. The capable and experienced worker has better reason to believe that effort will lead to success.

Exhibit A-2
Calculation of Choice of Effort Levels for Exhibit A-1

<u>1. Valences of first-level outcomes (primary outcomes)</u>

Formula: $V_{k.} = \sum_{i=1}^{m} I_{ki} V_{ki}$

$V_{1.}$ of successful performance: $V_{2.}$ of unsuccesful performance:

I_{1i}	V_{1i}	$I_{1i} V_{1i}$
1.00	.70	.70
.20	.90	.18
.50	.60	.30
1.00	.50	.50
	$V_{1.} =$	1.68

I_{2i}	V_{2i}	$I_{2i} V_{2i}$
1.00	.70	.70
.40	-.90	-.36
.70	-.60	-.42
	$V_{2.} =$	-.08

<u>2. Force to make effort and force to make no effort</u>

Formula: $F_p = \sum_{k=1}^{n} V_{k.} E_{kp}$

F_1 to make effort: F_2 to make no effort:

$V_{k.}$	E_{kp}	$V_{k.} E_{kp}$
.40	1.68	.672
.60	-.08	-.048
	$F_1 =$	.624

$V_{k.}$	E_{kp}	$V_{k.} E_{kp}$
1.00	-.08	-.08
	$F_2 =$	-.08

<u>3. Choice of effort level</u>

The effort level associated with the greatest positive force f_p is chosen. An interesting issue is raised if all forces F are negative. Will the smallest evil be selected or will no choice be made?

Appendix 2.

Hypothetical Example of Job Component Validity Computations

This example is based on a description of research conducted by McCormick, Mecham, and Jeanneret (1977). What we need to compute are the correlations between measures of worker characteristics, usually abilities, and characteristics of jobs (job components).

Our sampling unit in this endeavor is not an individual person, but a particular job. Exhibit A-3 shows the type of data that might be involved in computing these correlations. It simplifies matters by showing only 3 instead of 13 PAQ dimensions and by showing only 1 instead of 9 General Aptitude Test Battery (GATB) scales. The GATB is a test battery used by the U.S. Employment Service (U.S. Department of Labor, 1970). Given the data of a large number of sampling units (jobs), we could compute, as the exhibit is set up, the correlations between three job components and the GATB Clerical Perception scale.

The second part of the exhibit shows a correlation of .50 between Clerical Perception and clerical activities, based on data like those in the first part of the exhibit. It also shows correlations of 0.60 and 0.40 between Motor Coordination and machine operations and between Intelligence and decision responsibilities. These correlations are strictly hypothetical, designed to illustrate the validity of a psychological scale, GATB Clerical Perception, in predicting three job components that are involved in many jobs. The greater the weight of the job components measured by a particular GATB scale for a particular job, say that of file clerk, the greater the inferred validity of the scale for that particular job.

For example, the hypothetical correlation coefficient of .50 between the Clerical Perception subscale of the GATB and the "clerical/related activities" job component would indicate that the subscale measures the job component to some degree. Since we know from the top half of the exhibit that this job component is highly relevant to the job of file clerk, we might be inclined to infer that the Clerical Perception subscale is a valid test for selecting clerical workers. Evidence of this type suggests that the GATB as a whole is a valid measure for selecting people for jobs in general.

The statistics of job component validity are complex. The above interpretation assumes that validity is a characteristic of psychological tests, such as GATB Clerical Perception. McCormick et al. (1977) appear to be interested in the utility of the job components in predicting mean test scores of job incumbents in any job in order to define cut-off points that can then be used in personnel selection. This short discussion can only hope to serve as a stimulus to further reflection on this important topic currently attracting interest in psychological circles in a variety of guises.

Exhibit A-3
Computation of Component Validity Indices

(1) Weights of job components and mean GATB Clerical Perception scores

Job	Weight of PAQ job component			Mean GATB clerical perception (Q) scores
	decision etc. responsibilities	machine etc. operations	clerical etc. activities	
electronics assembler	2	5	3	2
file clerk	3	4	10	8
drill press operator	4	10	1	1

Note: It is assumed that the weight of a job component for a particular job and the mean clerical perception scores range from 0 to 10.

(2) Job component validity of three GATB subscales

Job component	GATB subscale	Correlation between job component and GATB subscale	Inferred validity of GATB for job category "file clerk"
decision etc. responsibilities	Intelligence	[.40]	3x{Intelligence}
machine etc. operations	Motor Coordination	[.60]	4x{Motor Coordination}
clerical etc. activities	Clerical Perception	[.50]	10x{Clerical Perception}

Note: The correlations in parentheses are outrageously hypothetical. The actual first-order correlations reported by McCormick et al.(1977) reflect complex relationships that do not serve the present pedagogical purposes.

References

Adams, J. S. (1965). Inequality in social exchange. In L. Berkowitz (ed.), *Advances in experimental psychology,* vol. 2 (pp. 267-299). New York: Academic Press.

Aeppel, T. (1983, July 14). Keeping the innovative spirit alive in companies. *Christian Science Monitor* (p. 85).

Anastasi, A. (1982). *Psychological testing.* 5th ed. New York: Collier Macmillan.

Baitsch, C., and Frei, F. (1980). *Qualifizierung in der Arbeitstätigkeit.* E. Ulich (ed.). Berne, Switzerland: Huber.

Baker, J. (1983, August). Contribution to N. Nisenoff (chair), *Setting the scene for working now and in the future.* Symposium conducted at the meeting of the World Futurist Society, Washington, D.C.

Baldamus, W. (1952). Type of work and motivation. *British Journal of Sociology* 2: 44-58.

Bales, R. F. (1949). *Interaction process analysis.* Reading, Mass.: Addison-Wesley.

Bandura, A. (1978). The self-system in reciprocal determinism. *American Psychologist* 33: 344-358.

Bandura, A. (1965). Influence of models' reinforcement contingencies on the acquisition of imitative responses. *Journal of Personality and Social Psychology* 1: 589-595.

Bell, D. (1973). *The coming of post-industrial society.* New York: Basic Books.

Bell, D. (1976). *The cultural contradictions of capitalism.* New York: Basic Books.

Bennett Mechanical Comprehension Test (1969). New York: Psychological Corporation.

Berg, I. (1971). *Education and jobs: The great training robbery.* Boston: Beacon Press.

Berg, I. (1974). "They won't work": The end of the Protestant ethic and all that. In J. O'Toole (ed.), *Work and the quality of life* (pp. 27-39). Princeton: MIT Press. Reprinted with changes from *The Columbia Forum* (1973, Winter), pp. 15-22.

Berlyne, D. E. (1960). *Conflict, arousal, and curiosity.* New York: McGraw-Hill.

Bernard, L. L. (1924). *Instinct.* New York: Holt, Rinehart and Winston.

Berrien, F. K. (1976). A general systems approach to organizations. In M. D. Dunnette (ed.), *Handbook of industrial and organizational psychology* (pp. 41-62). Chicago: Rand McNally.

Binyon, M. (1978, August 15). Eating out in Moscow. *The Globe and Mail*, p. 6.

Blake, R. R., and Mouton, J. S. (1964). *The managerial grid.* Houston: Gulf Publishing.

Bühler, K. (1924). *Die geistige Entwicklung des Kindes.* 4th ed. Jena, Germany: Gustav Fischer. Cited from R. W. White (1959).

Burke, R. J. (1982). Consequences of performance and competently executed work. *Canadian Psychology* 23: 73-83.

Campbell, D. T. (1977). *Manual for the Strong-Campbell Interest Inventory.* Rev. ed., Stanford, Calif.: Stanford University Press.

Campbell, J. P., and Pritchard, R. D. (1976). Motivation theory in industrial and organizational psychology. In M. D. Dunnette (ed.), *Handbook of industrial and organizational psychology* (pp. 63-130). Chicago: Rand McNally.

Carlyle, T. (1906). *The French Revolution, a history.* London: T. Nelson and Sons.

Cascio, W. F. (1982). *Applied psychology in personnel management.* 2d ed. Reston, Vir.: Reston Publishing Company.

Cattell, R. B. (1957). *Personality and motivation structure and measurement.* New York: Harcourt, Brace and World.

Cattell, R. B.; Eber, H. W.; and Tatsuoka, M. M. (1970). *Handbook for the Sixteen Personality Factor Questionnaire.* Champaign, Ill.: Institute for Personality and Ability Testing.

Cetron, M. J. (1983). Jobs with a future. In H. F. Didsbury, Jr. (ed.), *The world of work: Careers and the future* (pp. 189-199). Bethesda, Md.: World Future Society.

Chapanis, A. (1976). Engineering psychology. In M. D. Dunnette (ed.), *Handbook of industrial and organizational psychology* (pp. 697-744). Chicago: Rand McNally.

Chomsky, N. (1957). *Syntactic structures.* The Hague: Mouton.

Chomsky, N. (1972). *Language and the mind.* Enl. ed. New York: Harcourt Brace Jovanovich.

Clark, K. (1969). *Civilisation.* London: British Broadcasting Corporation and John Murray.

Cronbach, L. J. (1984). *Essentials of psychological testing.* 4th ed. New York: Harper & Row.

Davis, L. E., and Trist, E. L. (1974). Improving the quality of working life: Sociotechnical case studies. In J. O'Toole (ed.), *Work and the quality of life* (pp. 246-280). Cambridge, Mass.: MIT Press.

deCharms, R. (1968). *Personal causation: The internal affective determinants of behavior.* New York: Academic Press.

Deci, E. L. (1975). *Intrinsic motivation.* New York: Plenum Press.

Drucker, P. F. (1980). *Managing in turbulent times.* New York: Harper & Row.

Dubin, R. (1958). *The world of work: Industrial society and human relations.* Englewood Cliffs, N.J.: Prentice-Hall.

Dubin, R. (1973). Work and nonwork: Institutional perspectives. In M. D. Dunnette (ed.), *Work and nonwork in the year 2001.* Monterey, Calif.: Brooks/Cole.

Dukes-Dobos, F., and Henschel, A. (1971). *The modification of the WBGT index for establishing permissible heat exposure limits in occupational work.* Washington, D.C.: U.S. Public Health Service, ROSH, TR-69. Cited from McCormick and Ilgen (1985).

Dunnette, M. D. (1976). Aptitudes, abilities, and skills. In M. D. Dunnette (ed.), *Handbook of industrial and organizational psychology* (pp. 473-520). Chicago: Rand McNally.

Dürrenmatt, F. (1952). *Die Stadt, Prosa I-IV*. Zürich, Switzerland: Verlag der Arche, Peter Schifferli.

Emery, F. E., and Thorsrud, E. (1969). *The form and content in industrial democracy*. London: Tavistock Institute.

Emery, F. E., and Thorsrud, E. (1976). *Democracy at work*. Leiden, Holland: Nijhoff.

Engels, F. (1976). *Dialectics of nature*. (C. Dutt, trans.) Moscow: Progress Publishers.

Erikson, E. H. (1953). Growth and crises of the healthy personality. In C. Kluckhohn, H. A. Murray, and D. M. Schneider (eds.), *Personality in nature, society, and culture*. 2d. ed. (pp. 185-225). New York: Knopf.

Etzioni, A. (1961). *A comparative analysis of complex organizations*. New York: Free Press.

Evans, R. N., and Herr, E. L. (1978). *Foundations of vocational education*. 2d ed. Columbus, Ohio: Charles E. Merrill.

Eysenck, H. (1971). *Race, intelligence, and education*. London: Maurice Temple-Smith.

Feather, N. T., and Bond, M. J. (1983). Time structure and purposeful activity among employed and unemployed university graduates. *Journal of Occupational Psychology* 56: 241-254.

Fiedler, F. E. (1971). *Leadership*. Morristown, N.J.: General Learning Press.

Flanagan, J. C. (1978). A research approach to improving our quality of life. *American Psychologist* 33: 138-147.

Fleishman, E. A., and Berniger, J. (1960). One way to reduce turnover. *Personnel* 37: 63-69.

Freeman, R. B. (1976). *The overeducated American*. New York: Academic Press.

Frei, F.; Duell, W.; and Baitsch, C. (1984). Arbeit und Kompetenzentwicklung: Theoretische Konzepte zur Psychologie arbeitsimmanenter Qualifizierung. E. Ulich (ed.). Bern: Huber.

Fuller, J. G. (1975). *We almost lost Detroit*. New York: Reader's Digest Press.

Ghiselli, E. E. (1971). *Explorations in managerial talent*. Pacific Palisades, Calif.: Goodyear.

Gibney, F. (1982). *Miracle by design*. New York: Times Books.

Gilbreth, F. B. (1911). *Motion study*. New York: Van Nostrand.

Gilder, G. (1981). *Wealth and poverty*. New York: Basic Books.

Gilder, G. (1984). *The spirit of enterprise*. New York: Simon & Schuster.

Gooding, J. (1972). *The job revolution*. New York: Walker and Company.

Gorz, A. (1982). *Farewell to the working class*. (Mike Sonnenscher, trans.). London: Pluto Press.

Graen, G. (1969). Instrumentality theory of work motivation: Some experimental results and suggested modifications. *Journal of Applied Psychology Monograph* 53 (Whole No. 2, Part 2).

Greeley, A. M. (1972, April). The end of the movement. *Change* (pp. 42-47).

Hacker, W. (1978). *Allgemeine Arbeits- und Ingenieurpsychologie: Psychische Struktur und Regulation von Arbeitstätigkeiten.* E. Ulich (ed.). Berne, Switzerland: Huber.

Hackman, J. R., and Oldham, G. R. (1980). *Work redesign.* Reading, Mass.: Addison-Wesley.

Harris, M. (1981). *America now.* New York: Simon & Schuster.

Hendrick, I. (1942). Instinct and the ego during infancy. *Psychoanalytic Quarterly* 11: 33-58.

Herbert, F. (1978). *The Dosadi experiment.* New York: Berkeley Publishing.

Herrnstein, R. (1973). *I.Q. in the meritocracy.* Boston: Little, Brown.

Herzberg, F.; Mausner, B.; and Snyderman, B. B. (1959). *The motivation to work.* New York: Wiley.

Hilgendorf, L. (1966). Information input and response time. *Ergonomics* 9: 31-37. Cited from McCormick and Ilgen (1985).

Hinrichs, J. R. (1976). Personnel training. In M. D. Dunnette (ed.), *Handbook of industrial and organizational psychology* (pp. 829-860). Chicago: Rand McNally.

Hobbes, T. (n.d.). *Leviathan.* New York: E. P. Dutton.

Holme, R., and Perry, G. (1977). *Quality of life.* Poole, England: Blandford Press.

Hospers, J. (1967). *An introduction to philosophical analysis.* 2nd ed. Englewood Cliffs, N.J.: Prentice-Hall.

Hull, C. (1943). *Principles of behavior.* New York: Appleton-Century.

In the chips. (1982). Report of the Labour Canada Task Force on Micro-Electronics and Employment. Ottawa: Labour Canada.

Jackson, D. N. (1974). *Personality Research Form manual.* Goshen, N.Y.: Research Psychologists Press.

Jackson, D. N. (1982). *Jackson Vocational Interest Survey manual.* Port Huron, Mich.: Research Psychologists Press.

Jensen, A. R.(1969). How much can we boost IQ and scholastic achievement? *Harvard Educational Review* 39: 1-123.

Kabanoff, B. (1980). Work and non-work: A review of models, methods, and findings. *Psychological Bulletin* 88: 60-77.

Kalleberg, A. L.(1977). Work values and job rewards: A theory of job satisfaction. *American Sociological Review* 42: 124-143.

Kando, T., and Summers, W. (1971). The impact of work on leisure. *Pacific Sociological Review* 14: 310-327.

Knelman, F. H. (1981). The myopia of social systems. In G. E. Lasker (ed.), *Applied systems and cybernetics,* vol. 1 (pp. 183-190). New York: Pergamon Press.

Kornhauser, A. W. (1965). *Mental health of the industrial worker.* New York: Wiley.

Kruglanski, A. W.; Riter, A.; Amitai, A.; Margolin, B. S.; Shbtai, L.; and Zaksh, D. (1975). Can money enhance intrinsic motivation? A test of the content-consequence hypothesis. *Journal of Personality and Social Psychology* 31: 744-750.

Kuder, G. F. (1979). *Kuder Occupational Interest Survey, general manual.* Rev. ed. Chicago: Science Research Associates.

LaBenz, P.; Cohen, A.; and Pearson, B. (1967). A noise and hearing survey of earth-moving equipment operators. *American Industrial Hygiene Association Journal* 28: 117-128. Cited from McCormick and Ilgen (1985).

Landy, F. J. (1985). *Psychology of work behavior.* 3d ed. Homewood, Ill.: Dorsey Press.

Landy, F. J., and Trumbo, D. A. (1976). *Psychology of work behavior.* 2d ed. Homewood, Ill.: Dorsey Press.

Latham, G. P., and Wexley, K. N. (1977). Behavioral observation scales for performance appraisal purposes. *Personnel Psychology* 30: 225-268.

Lawler, E. E. (1973). *Motivation in work organizations.* Monterey, Calif.: Brooks/Cole.

Lazarus, R. S., and Monat, A. (1979). *Personality.* 3d ed. Englewood Cliffs, N.J.: Prentice-Hall.

Leont'ev (Leontyev), A. N. (1981). *Problems of the development of the mind.* Moscow: Progress Publishers.

LeShan, L. (1975). *How to meditate.* New York: Bantam Books.

Lewin, K. (1935). *A dynamic theory of personality.* New York: McGraw-Hill.

Likert, R. (1932). A technique for the measurement of attitudes. *Archives of Psychology*, no. 140 (1-55).

Likert, R. (1955). *Developing patterns of management.* New York: AMACOM.

Locke, E. A. (1969). What is job satisfaction? *Organizational Behavior and Human Performance* 4: 309-336.

Locke, E. A. (1973). Satisfiers and dissatisfiers among white collar and blue collar employees. *Journal of Applied Psychology* 58: 67-76.

Locke, E. A.; Shaw, K. N.; Saari, L. M.; and Latham, G. P. (1981). Goal setting and task performance: 1969-1980. *Psychological Bulletin* 90: 125-152.

Loevinger, J. (1957). Objective tests as instruments of psychological theory. *Psychological Reports* 3: 635-694. (Monograph Supplement 9.)

London, M.; Crandall, R.; and Seals, G. W. (1977). The contribution of job and leisure satisfaction to the quality of life. *Journal of Applied Psychology* 62: 328-334.

Luthans, F.; Paul, R.; and Baker, D. (1981). An experimental analysis of the impact of contingent reinforcement on sales persons' performance behavior. *Journal of Applied Psychology* 66: 314-323.

McClelland, D. C.; Atkinson, J. W.; Clark, R. A.; and Lowell, E. L. (1953). *The achievement motive.* New York: Appleton-Century-Crofts.

McConnell, C. R. (1984). *Economics: Principles. problems, and policies.* 9th ed. New York: McGraw Hill.

McCormick, E. J. (1959). Validity symposium: 3. Application of job analysis to indirect validity. *Personnel Psychology* 12: 402-413.

McCormick, E. J., and Ilgen, D. R. (1980). *Industrial psychology.* 7th ed. Englewood Cliffs, N.J.: Prentice-Hall.

McCormick, E. J., and Ilgen, D. R. (1985). *Industrial and organizational psychology.* 8th ed. Englewood Cliffs, N.J.: Prentice-Hall.

McCormick, E. J.; Mecham, R. C.; and Jeanneret, P. R. (1977). *Technical manual for the Position Analysis Questionnaire (System II).* Logan, Utah: PAQ Services Inc.

McDougall, W. (1923). *Introduction to social psychology.* 16th ed. Boston: John Luce.

McGregor, D. (1966). *Leadership and motivation.* Cambridge, Mass.: MIT Press.

McLellan, D. (1975). *Marx.* Glasgow: Collins/Fontana.

Maccoby, M. (1976). *The gamesman.* New York: Simon & Schuster.

Maier, N.R.F., and Verser, G. C. (1982). *Psychology in industrial organizations.* 5th ed. Boston: Houghton Mifflin.

Mankin, D. (1978). *Toward a post-industrial psychology.* New York: Wiley.

Mansfield, R. (1972). Need satisfaction and need importance in and out of work. *Studies in Personnel Psychology* 14: 21-27.

Marx, K. (1975). Economic and philosophic manuscripts of 1844. In *Karl Marx/Friedrich Engels Collected Works,* vol. 3 (pp. 229-346). New York: International Publishers.

Maslow, A. (1954). *Motivation and personality.* New York: Harper.

Matsui, T.; Okada, A.; and Mizuguchi, R. (1981). Expectancy theory prediction of the goal theory postulate "the harder the goals, the higher the performance." *Journal of Applied Psychology* 66: 54-58.

Meehl, P. E. (1972). Second-order relevance. *American Psychologist* 27: 932-940.

Miller, W. M., Jr. (1959). *A canticle for Leibowitz.* Philadelphia: J. B. Lippincott.

Mills, C. W. (1951). *White collar: The American middle class.* New York: Oxford University Press.

Mischel, W. (1968). *Personality and assessment.* New York: Wiley.

Mischel, W. (1973). Toward a cognitive social learning reconceptualization of personality. *Psychological Bulletin* 80: 252-285.

Mischel, W. (1984). Convergences and challenges in the search for consistency. *American Psychologist* 39: 351-364.

Misumi, J. (1972, August). *The validation of a conceptual model of leadership patterns.* Hakata, Japan: Kyushu University, Faculty of Education.

Misumi, J. (1982). *Meaning of working life: An international comparison.* Paper presented at the 20th International Congress of Applied Psychology, Edinburgh.

Mitchell, T. R., and Biglan, A. (1971). Instrumentality theories: Current uses in psychology. *Psychological Bulletin* 76: 432-454.

Murray, H. A. (1938). *Explorations in personality.* New York: Oxford University Press.

Murray, H. A., and Kluckhohn, C. (1953). Outline of a conception of personality. In C. Kluckhohn, H. A. Murray, and D. M. Schneider (eds.), *Personality in nature, society, and culture.* 2d ed. (pp. 3-49). New York: Knopf.

Needleman, C. (1979). *The work of craft.* New York: Knopf.

Orpen, C. (1978). Work and non-work satisfaction: A causal-correlational analysis. *Journal of Applied Psychology* 63: 530-532.

O'Toole, J. (ed.). (1973). *Work in America.* Cambridge, Mass.: MIT Press.

O'Toole, J. (ed.). (1974). *Work and the quality of life.* Cambridge, Mass.: MIT Press.

O'Toole, J. (1977). *Work, learning and the American future.* San Francisco: Jossey-Bass.

O'Toole, J. (1985). *Vanguard management.* Garden City, N.Y.: Doubleday.

Peters, R. S. (1965). Education as initiation. In R. D. Archambault (ed.), *Philosophical analysis and education* (pp. 87-111). New York: Humanities Press.

Peters, T., and Austin, N. (1985). *A passion for excellence.* New York: Random House.

Peters, T. J., and Waterman, R. H., Jr. (1982). *In search of excellence.* New York: Harper & Row.

Pinchot, G. (1985). *Intrapreneuring.* New York: Harper & Row.

Pirsig, R. M. (1975). *Zen and the art of motorcycle maintenance.* New York: Bantam Books.

Roethlisberger, F. J., and Dickson, W. J. (1939). *Management and the worker.* Cambridge, Mass.: Harvard University Press.

Rothery, B. (1972). *Survival by competence.* London: Business Books.

Rotter, J. B. (1966). Generalized expectancies for internal versus external control of reinforcement. *Psychological Monographs* 80, no. 1 (Whole No. 609).

Rousseau, J. J. (1961). A discourse on the origin of inequality. In *The social contract and discourses by Jean Jacques Rousseau* (G.D.H. Cole, trans.). New York: Dutton.

Rubinstein, S. L. (1977). *Grundlagen der allgemeinen Psychologie.* 9th ed. (H. Hartmann, trans.). Berlin, GDR: Volk und Wissen.

Ryan, T. A. (1970). *International behavior.* New York: Ronald Press.

Saleh, S. (1979, June). Some issues relating to intrinsic/extrinsic job orientation. In M. Morf (chair), *Competently executed work.* Symposium conducted at the meeting of the Canadian Psychological Association, Quebec City, Canada.

Sargent, S. S., and Williamson, R. C. (1966). *Social psychology.* 2d ed. New York: Ronald Press.

Sartre, J.-P. (1949). *Nausea* (Lloyd Alexander, trans.). New York: New Directions.

Schneider, J., and Locke, E. A. (1971). A critique of Herzberg's incident classification system and a suggested revision. *Organizational Behavior and Human Performance* 6: 441-457.

Schumacher, E. F. (1973). *Small is beautiful.* New York: Harper & Row.

Schumacher, E. F. (1979). *Good work.* New York: Harper & Row.

Skinner, B. F. (1957). *Verbal behavior.* New York: Appleton-Century-Crofts.

Skinner, B. F. (1971). *Beyond freedom and dignity.* New York: Knopf.

Smith, P. C. (1976). Behaviors, results, and organizational effectiveness: The problem of criteria. In M. D. Dunnette (ed.), *Handbook of industrial and organizational psychology* (pp. 745-755). Chicago: Rand McNally.

Smith, P. C.; Kendall, L. M.; and Hulin, C. L. (1969). *The measurement of satisfaction in work and retirement.* Chicago: Rand McNally.

Solzhenitsyn, A. (1963). *One day in the life of Ivan Denisovich* (R. Parker, trans.). New York: E. P. Dutton.

Stogdill, R. M., and Coons, A. E. (eds.) (1957). *Leader behavior: Its description and measurement.* Columbus: Ohio State University Bureau of Business Research, Research Monograph no. 88. Cited from Certo, S. C., and Applebaum, S. H. (1980). *Principles of modern management.* Dubuque, Iowa: Wm. C. Brown.

Tausky, C. (1978). *Work organizations: Major theoretical perspectives.* 2d ed. Itasca, Ill.: Peacock Publishers.

Taylor, F. W. (1911). *The principles of scientific management.* New York: Harper.

Terkel, S. (1972). *Working.* New York: Pantheon Books.

Thompson, G. B. (1979, June). Memo from Mercury: Information technology *is* different. Montreal: Institute for Research on Public Policy, Occasional paper no. 10.

Thurstone, L. L., and Chave, E. J. (1929). *The measurement of attitude.* Chicago: University of Chicago Press.

Tolstoi, L. N. (1942). *War and peace* (L. and A. Maude, trans.). New York: Simon & Schuster.

Toynbee, A. (1954). *A study of history,* vol. 8. London: Oxford University Press.

Trist, E. L., and Bamforth, K. W. (1951, February). Some social and psychological consequences of the longwall method of coal getting. *Human Relations* 4: 3-38.

U. S. Department of Labor, Employment and Training Administration. (1970). *Manual for the USES General Aptitude Test Battery, Section III: Development.* Washington, D.C.: U.S. Government Printing Office.

U.S. Department of Labor, Employment and Training Administration (1977). *Dictionary of Occupational Titles.* 4th ed. Washington, D.C.: U.S. Government Printing Office.

Vroom, V. H. (1964). *Work and motivation.* New York: Wiley.

Wagschal, P. (1978, August). Illiterates with doctorates: The future of education in an electronic age. *The Futurist* (pp. 243-244).

Weber, M. (1958). *The Protestant ethic and the spirit of capitalism.* (T. Parsons, trans.). New York: Charles Scribner's Sons.

Weber, M. (1968). *Economy and society*, vol. 3 (chap. 11) (G. Roth and C. Wittich, eds.; E. Fischoff et al., trans.). New York: Bedminster Press.

Weiss, D.; Dawis, R.; England, G.; and Lofquist, L. (1967). *Manual for the Minnesota Satisfaction Questionnaire.* Minneapolis: University of Minnesota.

White, R. W. (1959). Motivation reconsidered: The concept of competence. *Psychological Review* 66; 297-333.

White, R. W. (1960). Competence and the psychosexual stages of development. In M. R. Jones (ed.), *Nebraska symposium on motivation* (pp. 97-141). Lincoln; University of Nebraska Press.

White, R. W. (1976). *The enterprise of living: A view of personal growth.* 2d ed. New York: Holt, Rinehart and Winston.

Whitehead, A. N. (1929). *The aims of education and other essays.* New York: New American Library (Mentor Books).

Wilensky, H. L. (1960). Work, careers and social integration. *International Social Science Journal* 12; 543-560.

Woronoff, J. (1983). *Japan's wasted workers.* Totowa, N.J.: Allanheld, Osmun and Co.

Yankelovich, D. (1979). Work, values, and the new breed. In C. Kerr and J. M. Rosow (eds.), *Work in America: The decade ahead.* New York: Van Nostrand Reinhold.

Yankelovich, D. (1981). *New rules.* New York: Random House.

Author Index

Subject Index

About the Author

MARTIN MORF is Associate Professor of Psychology at the University of Windsor, Ontario. His earlier works have been published in *Behavior Research Methods and Instrumentation, Psychological Reports,* and the *Journal of Consulting and Clinical Psychology.*